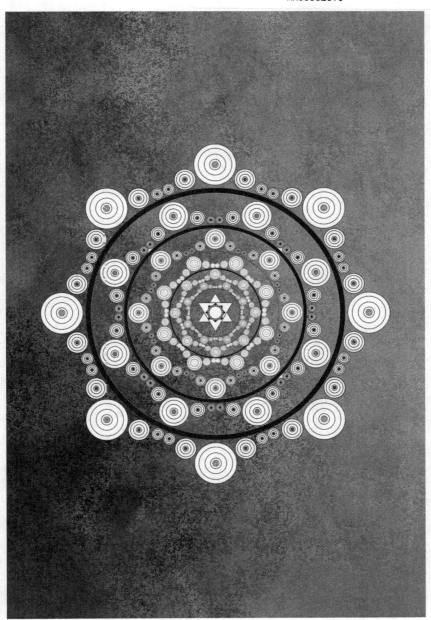

Dedication

I dedicate this book to the
empowering Presence that is our God Within.

The ever constant, encouraging
spark of Divinity that answers the call
of every question, every problem, every quest.

The unfailing love and wisdom
that takes us eternally higher
and leads us Home.

Acknowledgements

Since the release of my first book, *A Time of Change*, I've had the good fortune to talk with and meet many wonderful people dedicated to the empowerment and awakening of humanity. Male and female, young, middle-aged and old, naïve and wise, troubled and happy, they are opening their hearts and minds to Truth, willing to be participants and creators of a New World—a world that works for all and is based on Love, cooperation, harmony and peace.

I am privileged to witness their most intimate thoughts and feelings, their fears and strengths, their humanity. I can say with certainty that they are true people, loving and wanting to be loved, caring a great deal about our world and willing to learn and change.

It is because of them I had the opportunity to write this second book, Love, Miracles and Original Creation. Their dedication to growth has fueled many stimulating questions for Source, allowing for an incredible acceleration in wisdom and knowledge for us all.

I acknowledge them, and my beloved Ahonu, who worked tirelessly to prepare our weekly meetings with Source since 2009 to the present day. He edited and produced the recordings and the profound statements each week and did so with a smile and unfailing love for this work. Thank you my Beloved!

Without the many, I would not have seen these pages in print, nor would I have had the pleasure of sharing these experiences with the world. Unending thanks and blessings to all of you!

Aingeal Rose O'Grady - San Diego, CA, 2021

Table of Contents

Explaining the Levels	3
About The Akashic Records	10
God & Original Creation	17
Exploring DNA	32
Chakras	48
Kundalini	66
Consciousness	84
Time & Dimensions	106
The Future	122
Angels, Archangels & Ascended Masters	138
Our Light Bodies	160
Love	177
Miracles	199
Dreams	209
The Brain	238
Conclusion	259
About the Author	260
Bibliography	262
Index	263

Preface

We humans are an interesting conglomeration of races, nationalities, genetics and beliefs. Some believe we came from other planets and solar systems, making us aliens in human bodies. Ancient history suggests that our bodies were genetically modified by others from distant stars. Surely, we are still trying to understand how we were made, how the diversity of life (of which we are so intricately a part) came to be.

Nature itself is still a mystery—its power, intelligence and ability to continue to produce life and balance itself is quite remarkable, given the extreme attacks on it from toxins, fires, oil spills, pollutants, radiation leaks, chemtrails and weather modifications. To see orchids growing out of rocks and burnt ground producing lush, tropical foliage is quite miraculous.

How our bodies work is still challenging scientists. The answers to thought, healing, miracles, creation, consciousness, evolution and the purpose of life are still on the table for understanding. This second book from the Akashic Records (first was *A Time of Change* https://links.ahonu.com/atoc) continues exploring questions like those mentioned above. Understanding life and its purpose is revealed among these pages.

In exploring topics such as *God and Original Creation, Time and Dimensions, the Brain, Kundalini and the Chakras*, we have discovered our ascent into becoming God Man. We have understood the meaning and purpose of our lives, which encompass not only the delight of Creation itself, but the evolution of our nature into our God Presence and the joyful responsibility of being co-creators with one another and the forces of Nature.

We find how much we have underestimated ourselves and our potential and we see how we have turned ourselves inside out by focusing so much outside ourselves.

Source's consistent message throughout this book is to remind us of the rich internal environment of our body and consciousness. We see by these discourses that we haven't begun to touch the surface of our innate Divinity. The good news is that we have been given many ways to begin the discovery of ourselves; it can be done at any age and is not dependent on religion, race, upbringing or the past.

It is my desire that you will find joy and encouragement in these pages and that you will embrace your True Self in all its glory.

Thank you for sharing this journey with me!

Aingeal Rose

Chapter One

1) Explaining The Levels
2) Explanation of the Stairway
3) Explanation of Terms
4) About The Akashic Records

Explaining The Levels

In this book, we speak with Source on a wide variety of topics. Since the questions participants have asked are wide and varied, the answers cover levels ranging from the strictly mundane (or 3D perspective) to the deeply spiritual. Amazingly, there are core themes that run through each topic:

~ There is a Higher Plan in Creation
~ We are part of the carrying forward and success of this Plan
~ Each of us shapes our souls and contributes to the Whole

Throughout this discourse, you will hear talk about the negative agenda's (NA) plan vs. the Plan of God Source. This is to show the contrast between them and to discern the myriad of influences present in our world. This contrast leads us to the realization that these polarities exist within us as our 'split mind', which influences our brain-body composition. Since our outer world reflects our inner world, the decisions we make determine which 'plan' we are energizing. That we experience continual conflict with these aspects of ourselves is obvious.

Source has made it very clear throughout these transcripts that Its intention for all Creation is joy, freedom and the extension of Love. Therefore, correction at the level of the split-mind is necessary to manifest Source's intention in this world.

In response to some questions, you will hear Source say It has no opinion and yet, in response to other questions, Source will appear to have a strong opinion. This occurs when Source desires to get a message across to us of some importance that we can only grasp at our own level of understanding.

What may appear as a contradiction is really a deliberate attempt by Source to make a point at the level of comprehension of the one asking the question. In these cases, it is important to keep in mind the levels that are being addressed in response to specific questions.

To help us, Source has clarified terms such as Spirit, Individuated Spirit, Soul, Mind, Brain and Body in these ways:

Spirit—the essence from which all life is created, which is perfect in its composition or 'order', but *not* perfect in its *individuation* into the diversity of life forms. This imperfection is the result of the splitting off into various life forms, each having its own vibration. However, each life form is on its own evolutionary journey back to God Realization or 'Home'.

Individuated Spirit—the thinker, the decider, the observer. Because it is individuated, it has experiences and can perceive itself to be a separate self that can be injured and traumatized. This affects how it sees and thinks of itself for good or ill. This self concept or 'small ego' is at the level of the Individuated Spirit.

Soul—the accumulation or record of an Individuated Spirit's journey and evolutionary progress. The soul reflects the successes, victories or digressions of the individual. One can gain or lose soul energy by its victories or setback's through its various lifetimes.

Mind—the substance or 'plasma' which is the formative agent in the Universe. This substance is where ideas and concepts are converted into expressions that appear in what we perceive as 'outer' reality.

Brain—the *energetic* interface between the mind and body. It is a transmitter and receiver of information. The brain relays messages to the body from the Mind Field of the Individuated Spirit's concepts of itself.

An individual's self-concepts form into programs in the Mind Field (we sometimes found ourselves saying mine field !), which are relayed to the brain interface. The brain interface then transmits these to the body system, which translates them into chemicals, hormones and cellular compositions.

Body—the body is the matter expression of the Individuated Spirit and serves as a vehicle in this dimension for the purpose of experiencing, learning, expressing and affecting the quality of life in this density.

In understanding the cascade effect of this process, true and permanent healing can only occur from the level of the perceptions, beliefs, choices and conclusions the Individuated Spirit makes about itself and reality. The willingness to have the Higher Mind of God Source assist in the repair and correction of distortions in identity and perception is key to the success and evolution of the individual. Repairs at this level would naturally express its effects through all lower subsequent levels of soul, mind, brain and body.

I cover these subjects deeply in the *Answers From The Akashic Records* series (https://links.ahonu.com/aftar)

Explanation of the Book Image

Whenever I begin a new book, I always go into the Akashic Records and ask Source to give me the image to represent it. The image I received for this book was a set of stairs leading up the side of a golden pyramid which was surrounded by gold and silver spheres. The stairs led on through the clouds and up to the Sun.

Even though we have chosen a different image for the cover of this book, we quickly saw the importance of the stair-step image and had to mention it here. It is literally, the Stairway to Heaven.

The subject matter in this book unfolded to reveal our inner journey to becoming God Man. It explains the purpose for life and the amazing way it is constructed, ensuring that the potential for evolution and God Realization is inherent in the design of every life form, according to its level of evolution. We, as humans, are very fortunate to have an unlimited potential for awareness and ascension into higher realms of consciousness. We have the Presence of God within us, which allows for the potential for *biological* transformation and ascension.

The stairway image reveals this potential to become God-realized. The pyramidal structure has steps leading upward, showing us our path into our ascended 'Sun' state. The stairs are pink and white, indicating this path is one of purity of desire and intention. Indeed, purification is a major part of the success of this process.

That the pyramid is gold is no accident. It suggests that we become a permanent, refined essence—as indestructible and magnificent as God Itself.

The blue color beneath the stairs shows us the Truth that 'what is above is also below'; the structure of the pyramid journey has an inner counterpart, or complement, below the surface. On the way, we encounter parts of ourselves that need to be brought to conscious awareness and refined—the parts that are hidden from our conscious awareness. The blue indicates that the achievement of inner peace is an important part of our ascent.

Finally, the gold and silver spheres around the pyramid show us the perfect balance that is needed between male and female, electrical and magnetic, vertical and horizontal. This image also symbolizes the Mer-Ka-Ba geometries of which we are composed.

The Mer-Ka-Ba: History has talked about the Mer-Ka-Ba as the vehicle that allows a person to ascend or descend into the higher or lower worlds. Actually, the Mer-Ka-Ba is much more than just a vehicle of ascension. It can be really *anything*—since it is the primal pattern that created all things and all Universes, both visible and invisible (see *The Ancient Secret of the Flower of Life*, Vols. I & II https://amzn.to/3cTzweN).

In ancient Egypt, this primal pattern was called the Mer-Ka-Ba. It was three words, not one. *Mer* meant a kind of light that rotated within itself. *Ka* meant Spirit, in this case referring to the human spirit. *Ba* meant the human body—although it could also mean the concept of Reality that Spirit holds. The entire composite word in ancient Egypt referred to a rotating light that would take the Spirit *and* the body from one world into another.

Explanation of Terms

~~~

God—God Source, Creator, Source, All That Is, Prime Creator. All refer to the Originator of Love and Life.

Spirit—the *essence* of which all life is composed, which is perfect in its *composition or 'order'*, but *not* perfect in its *individuation* into the diversity of life forms.

Soul—the accumulation or Record of an Individuated Spirit's journey—its successes and challenges. Inherent in this is the Individuated Spirit's level of personal mastery; what it has gained or mastered on its journey to God Realization.

Mind—God's Mind

EGO—In the discussion on consciousness, Source defines EGO as our True Spirit Self. EGO being capitalized emphasizes our self-realized Identity.

Individuated Spirit—the thinker, the decider and the observer; it can be injured and traumatized. Because it is individuated, it has experiences that affect how it sees and thinks of itself for good or ill. A 'self concept' is made at the level of the Individuated Spirit.

Alter-ego—Source makes a point to describe our perception of ourselves as *alter-ego*. *Alter-ego* is used to define the small self or our made-up identity.

* * *

Mind Field—a substance of Creation that takes thoughts and ideas and turns them into concepts, allowing for perception to occur.

mind (small m)—the small self or alter-ego, denoting the identity we've made up to replace our true identity in God. True healing cannot occur at the mind level, as it is not the *originator* of concepts—the Individuated Spirit is.

Gravitational Collapse—the implosion of a star from its own gravity, resulting in a smaller and denser celestial object.

Collapse—a natural event caused by something suddenly falling down.

Implosion—a sudden inward collapse.

About the Akashic Records

Q. *What is Source's definition of the Akashic Records?*

A. The Akashic Records are a field of information appearing as streams of color, spheres of light, language, pictures, feelings, telepathic communication and body sensations. The Akashic Records encompass the collective unconscious where everything that ever was or ever will be resides. They are considered the *All That Is*. Once something occurs in Creation, it is added to the Field of the Akashic Records—in other words—it *exists*.

Q. *If time is simultaneous, how can anything have happened?*

A. Once something has happened, it is there. It doesn't have a distinction with time; it is part of the whole, which is timeless. It does not distinguish among past, present, or future—it just *is*.

Q. *What is the purpose of the Akashic Records?*

A. The Records are for God's pleasure and our pleasure. It is the same as asking "What's the purpose of existence?" They are one and the same. The Akashic Records are records of existence and existence is for God's pleasure and our own.

Q. *Are the Records open all the time or are some closed?*

A. God's information is open and free to everyone. There are no closed Records. However, if you are not at a sufficient level of consciousness, there are Records you cannot access or read.

Since they are a collection of *frequencies*, your ability to access the memory of the 'All That Is', is determined by your own level of consciousness.

Q. *Are there specific rules to access the Records?*

A. There are no rules *per se*, however, the Akashic Records are a field of *vibration* and accessibility is a function of your own motives and levels of awareness. Therefore, the 'rules' are—you can't access the Akashic Field unless you resonate at its frequencies.

Q. *Are there specific prayers to access the Akashic Records, or would an intention suffice?*

A. There is more than one prayer that can be said, but more than that, it is about your *purpose* for accessing the Records. Anyone with harmful intentions cannot access higher frequencies. The advantage of certain prayers is that they will uplift you to higher frequencies *temporarily*. Your ability to align yourself to those frequencies will determine how able you are to read the Records. Specific prayers do make a difference.

Q. *Are some people better able to access the Records than others, and if so, is the information coming through the same?*

A. Some people are better able to access the Records than others and this can affect the *translation* coming through in the down-stepping process. It depends on an individual's own filters of consciousness—their opinions and belief systems may taint the purity of what they can receive. You can teach a prayer to anyone and that prayer can help reach a higher frequency level, but how able a person is to *match* that frequency or down-step the information is a function of their own abilities. The exception to this would be to go into a hypnotic state similar to Edgar Cayce, where the perceptual filters are bypassed and not interfering.

Keep in mind however, that with the hypnotic process, the translator could be susceptible to wear and tear on his mind and body if he or she is not *naturally* attuned to higher frequencies.

Q. *Can you predict the future in the Akashic Records?*

A. In the Akashic Records you can see 'probable futures'. There are an infinite number of possibilities or timelines that all offer future potentials. When we see a probable future, it is showing a possible future outcome if no change is made. However, a probable future is not etched in stone—it is only a *potential* based on consciousness at the time the question is asked.

Q. *Can the Akashic Records be changed?*

A. No, they can only be *added* to. Let's say you could go back into the past to try to change an event. You'd find the original event is still recorded as it happened—you can't take something out of existence once it has existed.

What you *can* do is create a *new* event in a certain time period, but you are not taking away the old event. You are *adding* to the existing event or time period. This can be done because thought is creative, and in the realm of thought, time, space and distance do not exist.

It is easy to go to an event and create a new scenario with your mind. Because you are thinking and visualizing it, it is added to the Field as having happened. You have now created another possible timeline with a different outcome for that time period.

In the thought field, your visualization is being registered in the place or time of your intention.

Q. *Can you erase your own Records?*

A. No, you can't erase your own Records. Nothing is ever lost, but you can neutralize any *attachment* you may have to an event, time period, experience, person, *etc.* When we talk about erasing the Records, we are talking about neutralizing the 'charge' that's attached to a situation or event in the past. It forgives or reconciles the psychic energy or cords that you may have to certain aspects of your history. Some people call this 'karma'.

It is desirable to go back into your past and make peace with it. An event or situation is still recorded as memory, but there are no longer any cords or unforgiven issues. You don't erase it out of the 'Akashic Library', but you erase the *attachment*. By forgiving, you add another timeline and another time period to the event.

We're talking about the Records being *frequencies*. Any frequencies that lock parts of you in place or anchor you to certain events or time periods need to be reconciled. That way your time stream is clean—it becomes frequencies that looks like ribbons of beautiful, harmonious colors, as opposed to frequencies that would keep you locked in a place or time and cause you to reincarnate.

For example, you wouldn't want a prior lifetime still affecting you today, keeping you from being free. This is what is interesting about reading your own Records or your own 'Book'—you can see where you still have things to resolve. You can also see what you've *gained*. You can get a good measure of yourself.

Q. *Where are the Akashic Records located?*

A. Everywhere, throughout all existence. Even though the word *Akasha* implies a plane in Spirit, the truth is that the living field of information is recorded throughout all of existence, even in the cells of your body.

Q. *Are Records for different Universes in the same place?*

A. Again, it is about *frequency*. In one sense, you could say that everything exists simultaneously, but you wouldn't necessarily have *access* to every Universe if you are not vibrationally compatible to it. Records are contained within the fields where they resonate and have had experiences.

Q. *Can anyone access your personal Records?*

A. Yes, if they can access your frequency. No, if their intention is not honorable, or if there are lessons personal to you that need self discovery. In those cases, a blank wall of energy will appear, preventing them from reading your Records.

The Records have their own safeguard against persons whose intentions are not honorable in that such people's frequencies will not be high enough to access the Records. Anyone trying to read another's Records without their permission is not acting honorably. In principle, the Records are open books, but not in application. It is a perfect system.

Q. *Who are the 'Lords' of the Records?*

A. They are Beings whose job it is to guard the Records, meaning that they make sure each person's Records do not get mixed vibrationally with another's. They are *not* beings who bestow any kind of permission for us. The Records have their own safeguards against impure intent.

Q. *Is the name 'Lords' the appropriate name for these Beings?*

A. Yes, the name 'Lord' in this case means 'overseer' or 'guardian'. It does not refer to any kind of adoration or hierarchy.

Q. *How does that make sense if we're all One? Why would there be Beings to keep Records separate?*

A. Each Individuated Spirit is on its own journey to self-realization. You are misunderstanding 'One'. Oneness doesn't mean everyone dissolves into one thing. Oneness means 'in harmony with'. It means that you understand that everything is in relationship with everything else.

We all affect each other—its a unified field in that way—but it doesn't mean that we lose individuality.

* * *

Q. *Are there different levels of Records and if so, where are they and to what do they pertain?*

A. There are different levels of Records in that there are different Universes and differing frequency ranges in those Universes. The levels pertain to the experiences of those Universes wherever they are, but the information is accessible by anyone, anywhere.

Chapter Two

God And Original Creation

God and Original Creation

❦

Aingeal: "As I'm saying the opening prayer, I'm being transported upward into a vast field of crystal clear light, which is appearing as crystalline, undulating waves of light. I have a very ethereal and lofty sensation going all through my body."

Q. *How did Creation begin and will it ever end?*

A. I am being immersed in an incredible sea of lifeforce energy and vibration and I am being raised up higher and higher. I feel much Love—*so much Love* and I am also moving into a massive *place* of Love. I'm feeling such deep desire and Love. Creation has to do with Love and desire.

You can all imagine this with me. Imagine yourself floating in a sea of beautiful colors and waveforms. They are undulating and they are everywhere; beautiful undulating waves of light and color. As I'm moving into that, I'm feeling incredible love and desire. That's all I'm surrounded by.

Creation first came into being by Creator's love and desire. This feeling is very powerful and I don't see that it will ever end. *Once the desire for Creation was, it became a* **permanent** *intention and function.* It will never end and I am seeing more and more desire and more and more love. This is *intense* love; it is so incredible! I know I'm being repetitive, but I'm being immersed in this moment-by-moment experience! I'm using the word 'Creation' simultaneously with the word 'Life' because I am feeling the desire for life to be expressed, which is what Creation is.

Q. *Who or what is God Source?*

A. Please bear with me, because I am being transported to a very different frequency. I am moving into a gigantic white Sun. This Sun is pure white light. There is no yellow or red in it and it is not solid. I'm entering into this beautiful, huge, radiating sphere of white light, and now I'm entering a tunnel or hallway. I'm now in it and I'm walking down a hallway with rounded walls.

I can hear sound tones as I walk and the frequency here is making me shake a little. The intense feeling of love is bringing tears to my eyes. I'm hearing beautiful sounds that are echoing in my head, in my ears and in my breathing. There's a breath in this hallway as I'm walking, like a soft and peaceful rhythm. I am still in the tunnel, surrounded by this breathing rhythm that I'm feeling through every cell of my body.

I'm also aware of a reflective quality here, almost as if I'm surrounded by mirrors but I'm not. I'm aware that the sides of this hallway are reflective. I'm emerging now out into vast fields of beautiful, bright, white light. It is alive and I'm engulfed in millions and billions of eyes!

These eyes are dynamically alive and filled with awareness and presence. Every cell of my body is being penetrated by this. When we ask what God or the Creator is, this is what It is. It's this incredible brilliant white light that is filled with billions of eyes that are alive. It's not that these eyes are each separate beings —these eyes are One Creator. I feel such incredible love for everyone—incredible, never-ending love.

God is a being, but not limited as a being. God is dynamically aware and alive, pulsating, breathing and loving. It's everywhere and I see a smile now from this Presence, as if to say, "There's nothing to worry about, everything is Love; the intention is for bliss and enjoyment. Life and Love are the most important things. There is no judgment whatsoever." This Presence is not using language. As It desires, It vibrates Its intention into new Creations.

Q. *Where or how did God begin?*

A. God is laughing at me when I ask this question! God says, "I AM" and laughs uproariously. "I exist because I AM! How do you (meaning us) know you exist? You know because you *are*. No other explanation is needed." It began with consciousness, the awareness of the I AM.

Q. *Does God have a gender?*

A. What I hear Source saying is that there are billions of elements that make up Creation—much more than if you are masculine or feminine. Source encompasses masculine and feminine and much more. In this dimension, we are used to dividing things up into masculine and feminine, but that is very limited compared to what I'm seeing. I'm actually in the cells of God right now, in these billions of eyes and I can see and feel these billions of elements.

Source is saying, "I am masculine and feminine and much more. I AM all of it and I'm none of it." It is imparting to me that the diversities we call Life are filled with a myriad of colors and elements we've never seen before. Source is not identifying Itself with a gender, yet it encompasses all of it.

Q. *Is there more than one God? This question comes from the idea that there seems to be a different God for each religion.*

A. I want everyone to keep in mind that I am in a very different place/frequency here today—I am not answering these questions from an Earthly place or from any perception of an Earthly God—not Jehovah, not Allah, not Jesus, nor any of those beings because those are all Earth beings.

So, in answering this question, God is a *singular* Presence and this Presence has billions of eyes and every one of those eyes is God; they are not separate gods, but are part of One Presence that is an incredibly vast awareness. The gods of religions are not God, nor are they what I am seeing and feeling as God.

Q. *Is the God you're seeing and Prime Creator one and the same?*

A. Yes, It would accept being called Prime Creator in the context of what I've been seeing.

Q. *Did God create human life?*

A. Keep in mind again that I am answering these questions from this place of God's Presence. This Presence has striations of 'light' coming out of It as I answer this question. Source is saying, "You are all part of me." Imagine a vast Presence that has all these striations of light coming from It and every one of those striations is one of us. Source is gathering us unto Itself saying, "You are all part of Me," and every single pinpoint of light coming out of Its Presence is a different aspect of Its Creation. In other words, God's very being comprises us as well as everything else in Creation.

I'll go now to the human form question. It feels as if all Creation has come out of God's *heart* and I'm only using that word to describe the love that I'm feeling. Love is why we're here; Love is the reason we are all created and why *all* life has been created.

What I'm feeling about the human form and all the different forms of life everywhere (not just on our planet, but the diversity of life forms throughout Creation) is that they come into being through various combinations of elements, not specifically formed by God. There are many expressions of Creation that don't have physical forms like those in which we find ourselves. Many expressions are color, sound or geometry. There are so many different parts of God, but what I feel Source saying is that 'form' itself could never come into being if the underlying elements of God's intention were not in place.

All forms, shapes, geometries, light beings, etc., come from the elements, or substance of God, but God doesn't individually create forms. God is saying it doesn't matter if It deliberately created our human form or not; the fact is that all life forms are still composed of the elements of God from the simplest life form to the most complex. We are all gathered unto It and Source delights in all of it.

Did God deliberately create our human form? It's saying, "In the bigger picture, yes I did because you're composed of Me, but I did not directly mold you into your particular human form."

I hope you can grasp what I'm trying to say here. Source does not want us to focus so much on how our human form came to be, but more on the fact that we wouldn't exist at all if we were not made of God's Presence, which is Love. We humans have awareness and we have an ability to partake in Creation with God. It's about expressing love and love's desire and that is what God wants us to understand and realize.

Q. *Is Life itself intentional or accidental?*

A. Are you asking about Life as we know it here on Earth? In the big picture, Life is definitely intentional, as was already expressed. God's desire for Life and its expression is definitely intentional.

Life on Earth is also intentional because Source's intention is for Love to have unlimited expression and for Creation to be. This intention extends everywhere in the Universe. This intention is the lifeforce energy that allows life to come into being. It is the template behind everything. This loving intention manifests itself in a myriad of diverse, unlimited expressions. Every expression of Life has behind it God's intention for Life, otherwise it could never come into being.

Q. *Does God intend evil?*

A. No, God views evil as a distortion of Its intention. Its intention is clearly unlimited Love and desire for the pleasure, enjoyment and delight of Creation. The fact that people can take the elements and rearrange them, isolate them and use them to produce distorted things has nothing to do with Source. Source does not have a desire for that.

Source sees it as unfortunate that there are life forms that do not understand what the *I AM* is. (I just got this flash of the most beautiful colors and patterns you could ever imagine!) If we and other life forms understood the elements of God/Love of which we are composed, we would never be manipulating those elements in such a way as to create anything destructive. There is confusion about what God is and it's harder to remember what we're made of once we start rearranging elements in a destructive way. This applies to our thoughts as well.

Q. *Is there life on other planets?*

A. Of course. Life is throughout the Universe. Regarding life forms on other planets, some planets are teeming with life forms and other planets are not. There are planets that once teemed with life, but their inhabitants destroyed their environment, making their planet inhospitable. Some places once supported life forms and now they do not, but they will again someday.

What looks like a barren planet that once had life is really a planet that is in an internal process of regenerating itself. This process can take millions of years, but those planets will have life again at some point. I'm seeing how the Cosmos changes and Universes change—they may take billions of years, but they *do* change because the elements that compose the Universe rearrange themselves constantly. This process eventually develops new life forms. There are other planets in other Universes with civilizations on them that are similar to our own, while others are different. There is a wide array of Life everywhere.

Q. *Is the Sun a God?*

A. No. The Sun is a magnificent being that is also made up of the elements of God and I feel incredible love from it also. The Sun has self-awareness and it desires to contribute to the life forms in our Solar System. It is composed of elements that make it possible for other life forms to come into existence. It's a presence that is extremely loving and happy. It is a source of light, warmth, stimulation and regeneration. It would not want to be called 'God' because God is a word reserved for the Prime Creator. It's not appropriate to call anything else God, not even a highly advanced being. The word 'God' with a small 'g' is silly, really, because it reinforces separatist ideas.

The Sun has no problem being called a magnificent being of its own design or being appreciated for what its donation is, but in terms of being a God to worship, it's saying, "No, no, no!" It has consciousness just as much as a human life form does, except its shape is round and it is glowing. It is alive and aware. We can certainly have appreciation for the Sun and what it gives us. It would enjoy that!

Q. *What is the Holy Spirit?*

A. The Holy Spirit is the Presence of God within us and more importantly, it is the awareness of God within us. It is the remembrance of where we came from, what we're all about, what we're doing here and how to be in this world. It can also be considered our 'Higher Self'.

Q. *Does God hear our prayers or are we praying to our Higher Selves or to another entity?*

A. That's a great question! God definitely hears every prayer, and more than that, everything is *felt* by God. Once again, I'm in the upper levels speaking with this God Presence as I am answering this question.

Every form of expression is a cell in Its body, therefore, God feels every aspect of everything, every aspect of us. It feels every experience, every thought, every emotion and every plea.

Source is composed of such intense Love, desire and peace that every prayer is answered with this same Love, desire and peace. I feel it pouring unconditionally out of God's very Being. God does *not* respond to prayers by telling us what to do or by rearranging our lives for us.

Rather, It sends intense pulses of love, desire, peace and comfort to us which, when felt by us, increases our inner knowing and strength and puts us back into alignment with Truth, which *then* rearranges our lives. God answers us with a greater awareness of Its Presence. This filters down to the lower dimensions and causes the rearrangement of elements in our dimension. You could say it causes a change that we term a 'Miracle" (See Chapter 9 for more on Miracles).

Each pulse from God will manifest itself in a way that has to do with our particular combination of elements. Two people could be making the same prayer to God for a job, let's say. God's answer will manifest down through the levels and the form of expression it takes has everything to do with the individual persons' consciousness, how they perceive and believe and what they can accept. What means Love to one person may be totally different for another. For one, it could be a new job; for another it could be a relationship or a healing of some kind. This is where the Love of God will manifest the best it can, according to the makeup of the individual. God's answer is always to send out stronger and stronger pulses of powerful love, comfort and peace.

Q. *Some people seem to be answered immediately while others aren't. Is it because of the way God's Love gets filtered down through individual consciousness?*

A. Yes. When we come down into the lower density levels, we begin perceiving ourselves as separate and finite with our own personalities and beliefs.

The form a manifestation takes as it comes down through the levels will be according to our beliefs and what we can accept into our perceived reality.

Q. *How can we be sure that we are communicating with Source when we pray and not some other entity? Also, when someone prays to beings such as Jehovah, Budda or a Saint, does that prayer have the same impact as a prayer sent directly to God?*

A. Let's go to part one first. God is aware of every prayer and answers them all with the same Love. There's nothing God misses—that's how you can be sure. Answers that come from God are always loving answers. They are always based in Love and with them is a feeling of deep knowing and peace. All fear disappears immediately. You will feel there was never anything to worry about. You will feel it throughout your body and may even feel transported to a higher place in your consciousness.

For part two of this question—when people pray deliberately to a perceived god, saint or holy person, they will receive an answer based on the *quality* of the being they are seeking. In other words, you may feel peace from Buddha, judgment or command from Jehovah, love from Jesus, mercy from Allah and so on, whereas God's answer is always the same for everyone.

Q. *You mentioned in a former session that Jehovah is not the real God/Source. When someone prays to their perceived God, does their I AM Presence hear those prayers and respond?*

A. Yes, your own I AM Presence sometimes answers your prayers. If you are praying to a perceived god such as Allah or Jehovah or any other entity, Archangel or Ascended Master, you will receive an answer that reflects the likeness of that being. God Source does hear those prayers as well and will respond by sending Its pulse of Love to you, but if you're focusing on an answer from another being, you may only be receptive to an answer from the being of your focus. The *quality* of that being could be quite magnificent and its answer might well serve you or help you.

If you wait for an answer from Jehovah, for example, its answer may or may not be loving. We need to understand that when beings come into form, they each have particular qualities based on what they are and who they are. It's the same for us as well. Your own beliefs about gods or higher beings will determine the answers you can receive.

Q. *Why doesn't God just fix the Earth and the people on it?*

A. God is saying, "Why would I fix what you are creating?" It sounds like a simple answer, but it's really not. Source has told us It continually sends Its love, and it's such an incredible love! Its desire is always for love to be expressed. *We* create reality ,and we choose and create all sorts of scenarios. The fact that we see a world that needs fixing shows us that we have errors in our perception.

Imagine there are billions of thought waves with an infinite diversity of ideas and perceptions floating around. We are all continually thinking, imagining, perceiving, judging, loving, denying, sharing, restoring life, killing, giving birth, dying, etc. All these things coalesce into unique forms of expression on a variety of levels. These forms may unravel at some point or they may stay in their form of expression by the focus of consciousness.

Source is not interested in rearranging our creations or making them appear all nice and neat for us. Our world and our experiences are *our* creations of consciousness. We were given life to be able to express as we wish. We are free in that way. If we don't like what we have formed as a result of our consciousness, *we* are the ones to unravel it and make it different.

Each aware being has the responsibility for the quality of what it manifests with its thoughts and desires. We each are in charge of our lives because we have the self-awareness to do so. We can think, decide, observe, feel, invent, inspire, change our minds and connect with Source. We are blessed!

God plays Its part by reminding us that at the *core* of everything, Love is all there is and is what's most important to uphold. It is a *standard* to live by—a quality to uphold—the Truth and the answer to every question. If we want to use our thoughts and actions to create other than that or to judge, condemn others or find them guilty, make a mess of the environment, we are free to do so. It will not be God's fault, nor is it God's responsibility to fix it. It is *ours*. We can turn it all around and have it be a blissful existence whenever we are ready. It could be an instantaneous shift.

It's easy to focus on what's wrong or look at things and not see Love. What we see 'out there' is a decision we each make with our perception. In God's Presence, Love is still in existence and will always be constant, sure, patient and accepting. Love is never going to be affected by anything we do with our consciousness. We can destroy a planet and put ourselves through all manner of suffering for as long as we choose. God knows that at some point in our existence, we will change our minds and be tired of our foolish use of consciousness. So, you can see why God is not interested in taking away our beautiful creative powers and freedom to express and experience, which It would be doing if It suddenly rearranged our world. It would be taking away our power of creating it all! We are free to rearrange the elements of our physical world with our consciousness and change what we experience. It's the delight of Creation to create.

Q. *Are we here to learn lessons?*

A. Many people believe that, but Source says, "No, we are here to experience bliss and joy." It may seem we are here to learn lessons because we are on a path of awakening to our True Presence, which might also be considered *evolution*. Evolution will eventually result in the realization of Source's intention to experience bliss and joy, which is to *be* the Love that we are, to understand what '*we as God*' means. To *be* Love itself with no fear.

What appear as 'lessons' are really a gradual path of awakening from the dream of the necessity for suffering and hardship. We create our own hardships by the *content* of our beliefs. If there is a lesson to be learned it is, *'Like attracts Like'*. We will experience what we believe. God does not give us lessons —God gives us more and more Love until we get it that Love is the only true reality.

Q. *I pray for those I love and for those that have passed on. Is there more I can do?*

A. It's a really good question because *some* people who cross over do not go to the light right away and experience the Love we've been talking about. Some are stuck in astral planes out of fear of Gods judgment or an inability to accept that they have died. Any prayer you send is helpful. It provides grace for them to be able to move on.

We have forgotten the Love that is God that *we are composed of*. We've really confused things here, but sending someone heartfelt Love or a blessing is opening the door for a Miracle. When someone gives and receives Love, it opens the potential for a miraculous shift and a miraculous rearrangement of elements.

Q. *Do we have the ability to manifest our own desires? Can we feel connected to Source continually?*

A. You can create anything you can believe and imagine. When you have a desire and you apply deliberate and focused intention for manifesting, the elements of creation start to rearrange themselves into the form of your desire. So, yes, you have the ability to change your environment. The success or failure of your manifestations or lack of them is determined by how clear you are at the level of your subconscious mind, your soul contract and your motivation for your intention. In other words, why do you really want your desire?

Feeling your connection to Source is really dependent on how willing you are to see only Love everywhere. Since God is only Love, making that your *only* intention and purpose brings you closer and closer to that experience. Yes, it is possible to feel God's Love everywhere and to see God's Love in everything, but it is a choice. We need to release the belief in anything other than pure Love, joy and bliss.

Chapter Three

1) Exploring DNA
2) Chakras
3) Kundalini

Exploring DNA

Q. What is Source's definition of DNA?

A. I am looking at small squares of white light and I am seeing that the DNA is the building block of Creation that follows a sequence or pattern. One block seems to build upon the next and the next, like a chain. We've seen this image of DNA that Science has shown us, so that's no surprise. Source is saying, "DNA is literally the 'chain of events'." It is formed and unfolds in its diversity of forms by the sequence of events that have taken place in particular areas of the Universe. DNA strands are woven patterns of light with varying informational sequences in them, occurring through the process of adaptation and experimentation. Contained within it is the record of a life form's *history and evolution*.

Our own individual DNA is based on *historical events* encoded throughout time. It comes into being or 'builds itself' by what is coded within it and it has an evolutionary process to it. As I go back further toward Source, DNA itself seems to *reflect* an original pattern of Creation built upon different molecules.

Q. What is the potential and purpose of DNA?

A. DNA has unlimited potential for expansion and change because it is built upon sequences of events that can change and alter its chemical composition. I am watching a collection of ribbons of light that intertwine and carry specific information. Its purpose is to establish patterns for life forms to be.

In its history is its evolution and without that information, a life form wouldn't know what to be or how to form. In its codex of information and history is contained the intelligence to unfold a particular life form.

I'm seeing light, colors, chemicals, hormones and other aspects of cells that are all coded inside DNA with quite complex information. As I'm looking at it, I see a glistening white crystalline moist gel-like liquid structure that has a *reflective* quality to it. This makes me feel that it is alive, with living and breathing lifeforce energy.

Q. *How many strands or ribbons of color make up the DNA?*

A. Since the DNA is a latticework of information, the number of strands contained within a particular life form corresponds to the evolution and type of life form. The number of strands is different for each particular life form. For a human being, we've been at a 2 to 3 strand *activation* of DNA for a very long time. Activation determines the amount of strands that are actively alive and functioning. Even so, our specific coding can be altered and changed. Source says that we currently have a 12-strand *potential*, with the 13th potential also encoded. 'Potential' implies evolutionary capability, meaning we can activate and 'turn on' 12 strands of DNA within our biology.

We are meant to evolve and actualize up to 12 strands and once that happens, we have the potential to activate a 13th strand. At that point, this will make us a very different biological life form. We do not have 12 strands *activated* at this time.

Currently, we have the potential to turn on our 4th, 5th and 6th strands of DNA. We've been at a 3 strand activation for many millions of years and now many people are having their fourth strand turned on. With the cosmic awakening process we are now in, some people will activate their fifth and sixth strands. If we can do that, we will be able to retrieve our higher gifts and abilities such as telepathic awareness and communication, pastlife recall, perceive subtler energies and have X-ray vision.

We will also gain the ability to move between dimensions, have the potential to understand consciousness at a much more expanded level, experience telekinesis, teleportation, bi-location and the heightened expansion of our senses.

This is a great answer from Source because it puts things in perspective. If we were to activate our seventh and eight strands, for example, which we *aren't* doing right now, we'd be moving into higher aspects of our own God nature. In the session on Kundalini, which is in a later chapter, we see that this activation process is also a purification process up the Chakra system. The potential is there within us to become God Man and this has to do with the activation of our 12-strand potential. Once this is achieved, we have the potential to activate the 13th strand, at which point we'd become an entirely new type of being. As you can see from where we are currently, we still have a long way to go. We will be waiting for another Stellar Activation Cycle to occur after this one, which will afford us the opportunity to activate strands 7 through 12. The potential for the activation of the 13th strand will occur after that. Each Stellar Activation Cycle allows for an increase of light and activation, which provides the potential for awakening and quickened evolution and adaptation.

It is true that individually, in-n between Stellar Activation Cycles, we can still activate our own DNA by doing our own purification process. This process can take many lifetimes, however. Stellar Activation Cycles provide us opportunities for accelerated activation and growth.

We can see this process happening in our world today. Much darkness is being exposed and people are waking up worldwide, but this process also involves the conflict between the old order and the new. Think of all the things we are trying to change. We need to respect Nature and all life, we need to stop suppressing the rights of the individual; we need to uproot dogmas that enslave the human being. We also need to stop condemning criminals to death. We need to stop killing our environment and our food.

We have much to do and we can see how this change will still take many years. Our own alter-ego will challenge us. If we remember that DNA is built by *historical events*, we can see that *we* are a mixture of the events of history which contains both light and dark. History is part of our own anatomy and has to be purified or forgiven *through* us for true evolution to occur. Until this is done, we will only see small evolution and repeats of the past.

Q. *What happens when DNA strands are activated?*

A. First, DNA carries potential for activation because history can change. Since you were born, new histories have been occurring throughout the Cosmos, which means the next generation will have different information in their DNA than we have. They will have old history and new history. There is an alchemical change that occurs because the DNA is about information and in its activation, the DNA spiral itself receives the new information. You can say that the DNA strands receive new light codes, but what they really are is new history coming from the Cosmos, which translate to new information. Once the DNA receives new information, it starts to change the chemicals and hormones according to those activations, causing a biological evolution of the species.

Q. *We hear of people who are offering 22-strand DNA activation through the use of crystals and specific ceremonies. What is actually happening in these ceremonies?*

A. The first thing Source is saying is that we do not have a 22-strand DNA potential in our current human form. A 22-strand being is a very huge presence that is very much out of our Solar System. Even though our DNA potential is unlimited, in our current biological state we have a 12-strand potential, which in and of itself is still quite huge when you consider the gifts and abilities that go with it.

There is no fast track to that type of evolution. Anyone who promises to activate 22 strands of DNA has been misinformed. If this were available to us, we would all be turning into light bodies. The ceremonies performed, however, can do a limited degree of DNA activation by bringing in higher light codes, which begin to restructure specific geometries in the body and cause subtle changes in the light body. In any activation, the people being activated still have to be able to maintain and integrate those frequencies within their body and consciousness. It is one thing to have something *catalyze* a change and quite another to integrate that change into your biology. We need to keep in mind what this particular Stellar Activation Cycle affords us and that is the activation of our fourth, fifth and sixth strands of DNA.

Q. *In our current human form, are our genetics fixed?*

A. No, they are not fixed based on what we've been shown. Let's go back to explaining how the DNA is formed and how it changes through history. Without this history and without the *information* in the history, a life form would not take its shape and form. The genetics we inherit from our parents are the building blocks for our particular body. This holds a pattern of information that determines what gets passed down from parent to parent, person to person. But here's where I want to put things in perspective; the DNA is alterable. It is not fixed in the sense of the DNA you were born with. You don't have to accept that there's nothing you can do with your DNA for the rest of your life. We just explained how the DNA could evolve by activations, but it also evolves by consciousness and emotional changes.

If no changes are ever made in consciousness or emotions, there will be nothing to catalyze your genetic pattern and thus it may stay in place for the duration of your life. However, if you become more conscious or are being activated by the current Stellar Activation Cycle, the potential for the evolution of your DNA and therefore your individual genetics, is very strong.

Its an evolution that's going on now. It's easy to see the effects of this process in the new children that are being born today. They are coming in with more DNA strands turned on. Most of them have 4-6 strands activated with their added abilities and gifts. So, your genetics are fixed while your biological form is being created, but once you start working with your DNA, it can be altered by shifting emotions and consciousness. You're creating a new DNA structure which is unique to yourself and that will be passed on generationally or genetically if you have children. Whenever we evolve to a higher level, that potential can be passed genetically.

Q. *I have been doing ancestral DNA research on my family and was told by someone I respect that this kind of work clears seven generations back and forward. Could Source explain this?*

A. What Source is saying to me is that the DNA changes when we clear negativity and our lower nature thoughts, beliefs and emotions. Our diet contributes on a very small scale, but we're really talking about a purification process *in consciousness*. Source is saying we cannot clear things for our relatives backwards and forwards because we have to take into account individual soul journey's. The work of mastery is personal. Think of all your ancestors—they are having their own relationship with their own soul and Spirit. Another person can't magically clear karma for them.

However, we *can* be a force that catalyzes and purifies ancestral patterns in ourselves and thus affect future generations genetically. Each Spirit has its own challenges so that it can become more masterful and victorious. When we shift our own DNA, we offer higher energy and higher consciousness to our ancestors and to the world.

If I were to research the patterns that show up in my own family's DNA over the centuries, I might be able to notice recurring patterns and thus be able to see how those patterns are evidencing in my life today.

With that information, I would know better what my choices need to be around those patterns. In this way, I have the potential to alter a pattern that's been in my family history for generations.

When we think about the past and about ancestors and relatives who have passed on, we're not really altering *their* DNA because DNA is a physical thing in the body and these people are no longer physical. What we are doing is ending particular patterns and providing new potentials for future generations.

Let's say you've got someone in your family who is making choices that are not the healthiest, or there may be an unhealthy aspect of the DNA that's causing issues. You may be offering some higher coding for them so that they can receive more light, which has the potential to awaken them, but you don't necessarily correct the issue for everybody in your family line.

However, here's the exception: It goes back to the story of Jesus. The Christian belief is that Jesus died for our sins on the cross. The implication is that he wiped out the sins of humanity. In essence, he purified the human race through the forgiveness of their karma. There is a fundamental truth in the story, even though there are some who claim that Jesus never existed. It doesn't matter if he lived or not because the *principle of forgiveness* is the point. It's a principle that says it only takes one person who truly realizes the Love of God and the innocence of all brothers and sisters to completely purify the human race. The idea of Jesus shedding blood is the symbolic idea of releasing an old DNA program and replacing it with a resurrection program.

The resurrection program is that everyone is forgiven and deserves love and is continually given this love by Source without fail or end. Only the *actualized realization* of this purifies the old genetic code of guilt and punishment. So, if Jesus did exist, he could have completely forgiven the world. This would mean that all effects of karma are forgiven and that all bloodlines have been purified. So, we look around and see that there is still suffering going on, people are still struggling, people are still behaving in ways that are criminal, our own thought processes are still both positive and negative.

It doesn't look as if all has been forgiven because we still 'sin' and we are still punished in this world. Here's the point; each person has to *choose* to acknowledge that they've *never been guilty*. Each person has to come to the awareness of his or her own innocence and that Love is the truth of God. Each person has to become completely harmless within themselves to the point that they have no desire to judge another and wish only to give love to everyone equally. It's easy to see that this is the work we all need to be doing.

Only when this happens will we have completely changed the DNA patterns of our ancestors and those to come. This is why those who believe in the story of Jesus can say he is their savior. This kind of Love is what releases everyone from the bondage of guilt and judgment, which releases karma. Has everything already been forgiven? Does our DNA hold this truth? *Yes, it does* and we have only to accept it. Until we do, we won't see it evidenced in our outer world. You don't have to believe in Jesus for this to be true. It is true because this is what Source is and does.

Q. *What is the relationship between DNA and Karma?*

A. Remember, DNA is a 'chain of events', therefore the DNA holds the karmic imprints from the past within it's coding. Karma is the set of imprints that are being transferred from generation to generation or from lifetime to lifetime. It carries not only parental information, but also the information of our other lives once our spirit enters the body vehicle formed by our parents.

We will see these patterns repeat themselves through generations until we understand that love and innocence are the same thing. As long as we believe in Karma as a balancer of evil or good, we will not understand forgiveness and the Love of God. We can now understand why it takes many thousands of years for anything to change at the DNA level. Evolution has occurred slowly because consciousness hasn't changed much throughout the centuries.

There is also a strong ancestral loyalty which follows through generations. This loyalty, whether healthy or distorted, is one of the blockages to work through in evolving centuries-old ancestry.

Q. *Does human DNA contain alien or extraterrestrial DNA?*

A. That question is taking me into a totally new place. I'm feeling an opening into a bright light that I'm breathing in. Source is telling me that our DNA originally was a pure blue white spiral flame. It feels extremely clean, pure and powerful. Our original template came down from Source. I'm being taken back to the beginning of the original template for all life, which came from the spiral of Source. What It wants us to know is that the original life-force template has been very much 'nullified'. I find that an interesting word because it implies that our DNA has been altered to such a degree that much of the original power and force we carried is no longer present. Source wants to make it clear that originally our DNA spiral was modeled after something Divine, but it has digressed since then.

Up to now in our discussion, we've been talking about our human form, which has a 12-strand DNA potential contained within it. At this time, we have to climb back up the ladder (those steps, again) to *activate* our 12 strands through the purification of our lower or 'fallen' nature. Activation needs to be integrated now in steps. In other words, when we reactivate certain strands, we will then have the potential to reactivate more and then more. However, Source wants to be clear that this process of ascent is still a very down-stepped version of our current human DNA, compared to the potential that we had originally. Things have become so far regressed that our process of bringing our DNA back online has been a slow process of evolution with some help from the various Stellar Activation Cycles. Even when these cycles come along, we have made only slow progress, as the shadows within us have kept us enslaved. Hopefully, we will make much more progress this time.

Regarding human DNA containing alien DNA, biologically we are a combination of many ET races. Our DNA is encoded with this historical information. The alien mix has resulted in the chemical compositions of our bodies. This DNA chemical composition is weak compared to the potential of Source within us. Even though we've been altered by having our higher-center DNA strands shut off, our potential to evolve into a God Man is still very real. Our cross-breeding with other life forms and animals long ago has left us with a lower, animal nature mixed with a higher, God-like nature. This is why we have the task of purifying our lower nature so we can recover our higher nature. The original imprint of Source is still biologically within us as well. If it weren't, you wouldn't have any possibility for life at all. This original imprint is still much stronger than any impurities of cross-breeding that occurred long ago.

Here's a small example of what part of this process looks like biologically; we have a lower portion of the brain that is considered the reptilian brain, which is also called the 'pons'. Currently, it has too much influence within our brain. It carries a type of dominance that makes us aggressive, reactive and warlike. Yet, there are certain brain exercises we can do that will develop higher brain pathways and reduce the reptilian portion of the brain so that the evolution of our DNA can occur. The higher brain is what bridges the gap between God Realization and us. I am describing God in this example as higher intelligence, genius mind, inspiration, clarity, energy and solutions to all problems. This is only one small example of the task at hand. The good news is that new brain pathways can be developed at any age.

Q. *Regarding reincarnation, could we have been our own ancestors in another life?*

A. Yes, it's definitely possible that you could have been your own ancestor in another life.

Q. *Is Twin Flame DNA the same or similar in each partner?*

A. Yes, and no. Your DNA is not the same because *biologically*, as a physical person, each one of you comes from different parents, making your physical bodies unique. However, once your spirit selves enter the body and your soul history becomes encoded in your DNA, you will find similarities there. To help with this process, each of you would have chosen as part of your soul contract, to be born into the physical family that would best serve your relationship and soul evolution.

Twin Flames are truly connected because they are the same *spirit* and this is what needs to be understood. At this level, you're not a body at all; rather you are one spirit flame. You don't have DNA—you are pure spirit twins who are the same spirit. Once this original flame splits and each part begins incarnating into different life forms, each will take on a different pattern and a different history. Still, when they meet one another in particular lifetimes and they remember that they *are* each other, they may find that they have had very similar experiences in their individual sojourns through time and space. Twins are always connected energetically because they're the same spirit. What one experiences in a lifetime, oftentimes the other will also have had experienced something similar in their lifetimes. This doesn't mean that they'll necessarily remember each other's past lives, but they may! They could very well remember incarnations that they spent together.

Many times, Twin Flames have the same unhealed wounds and some of the same spiritual experiences. Whatever they experience in their 'separate' incarnations, the other is affected by and vice-versa. The exception to this answer is if the Twin Flames were born into the same family as *biological* twins, then they would share the same biological DNA.

Q. *Is it possible to change a DNA coding of poverty? If so, how?*

A. Part of what we're doing in this cycle is purifying mass consciousness beliefs. It isn't just about ourselves—many people around the world have inherited poverty patterns.

Ahonu and I were talking about what the martyr complex means within mass consciousness and within ourselves as individuals. As a society, we still very much believe in victims and victimizers, which equates to beliefs in guilt and punishment. If someone commits a crime or behaves badly, the victimizer is to be punished and the victim is innocent. This thinking is very pervasive. We aren't only clearing our family patterns, we're also clearing centuries of old paradigms. We're all a part of that and we've all agreed to it. Poverty consciousness is one type of mass-consciousness belief. It goes along with the victim-victimizer mentality and the beliefs in guilt and punishment.

It is very possible for you to clear these beliefs in yourself, however all changes require decisions and choices about what you want to believe is true for you. Poverty is the human belief in victim-victimizer because God's will is abundance, which is evidenced everywhere in Nature. Every spring we see the evidence of abundance. We see the billions of seeds that get carried on the wind by trees, plants and flowers of all varieties. Hundreds of pinecones are created and fall to the ground each year from one tree alone. Look at all the new buds and blades of grass. This abundance and plenty is the natural state of God's will. When we're experiencing something other than this, it is because we still hold beliefs within us that make us think that we are unworthy or that the supply is limited.

If you had parents or grandparents brought up during the depression, you may have inherited their fear that there isn't enough. It is still possible to shift those inherited ideas. It's a diligent choice. In other words, you have to watch yourself and look at where you're going with your thoughts and the experiences in your life. Your experiences are *symbolic representations* of your thoughts.

Source would like to get across that the foundation of life is love and love is abundance, happiness and expansion. It's unlimited potential. You can clear poverty conscience when you take a look at your beliefs and experiences that are contrary to love. Take a look also at your desires and intentions towards yourself and others. Ultimately, everything comes down to the perceptions you have of yourself, others and life.

Source has said that you don't have to go back and remember other lifetimes, but you can be shown some of them for informational purposes. You can simply look at your present life and see what's occurring in your day-to-day experiences. Those are your patterns and limitations and it doesn't always matter where they came from. You can still undo them in the present. Make a different decision and redefine what things *mean* to you. Turn a negative perception into a positive one—they will register in your subconscious as new programs.

Q. *Did we emerge from sea creatures?*

A. Many humans did live in the sea at one time, but that's not all that happened. We were also genetically changed at different time periods. Some of the species that evolved to be our particular type of form were implanted with higher-potential DNA codes from other advanced races, causing a quantum jump in evolution. Others came later and altered the DNA in such a way as to regress our potential, as mentioned earlier.

Some of us have spent time in the sea and may have a memory of being a particular sea creature. Others may remember the sea, but may not have been sea creatures. Life in the sea is part of our DNA history. This is why we can also remember being from another dimension or planet.

Some of us belong to advanced races that came here very long ago and put their DNA into the animal-like creatures here to evolve them. We are talking about a wide expanse of evolutionary history covering billions of years.

Some of us were those original beings who upgraded DNA; some of us could have been those who came later and down-stepped the biology, making a portion of our DNA dormant. This is why it is now necessary for us to 'resurrect' ourselves as a species.

Q. *How can our DNA potential be activated more quickly?*

A. We can meditate with our DNA. We can see it in our mind's eye and talk to it. Practice asking it questions and waiting for an answer. Source is saying that the highest way to change your potential is to change your *purpose* into becoming *only* love. It is about the desire to be only love, compassion, understanding and harmlessness. It's choosing the state of consciousness where your higher gifts naturally unfold, which is the evidence of your evolving DNA.

Q. *Do the foods we eat suppress or activate our DNA?*

A. What I hear Source saying is that food does not directly change our DNA. The DNA changes by evolution/adaptation. It needs to evolve to a different frequency entirely. Think about food in terms of providing nutritional building blocks to the body. Food can contribute lifeforce energy to the body, which gives it the ability to process life and keep the immune system strong. Food provides light and energy, but it doesn't directly change DNA. Source has talked to us many times about food and we each have to find out which foods are right for our particular body. Whatever type you are, stay away from GMO and processed foods. Buy organic vegetables, grass-fed beef and butter, free-range chicken and eggs and good quality oils. The brain needs fats to think, so avoid foods that are low fat. Eat good quality oils from coconut or nuts. Reading labels on food products is always a good idea.

Q. *Is it possible for a healer to change a person's DNA?*

A. A healer or energy worker can bring more light into the body of a person which can activate some DNA changes by bringing in more light, depending upon the quality of it. However, the only way that's going to become a permanent change is when the recipient can hold the activation. The individual being treated must maintain this shift in frequency in order to have a permanent DNA activation.

In the story of my own spiritual evolution, I had two things happen. I meditated every day and I was taken into many different worlds, which raised my frequency. These worlds held paradigms which were more loving and cooperative than here in Earth. I had to incorporate these paradigms within myself in order to maintain the higher frequencies. I was taught about inner purification and I had to do much inner work to examine myself and forgive when necessary. As you can well imagine, this is an ongoing process.

I was also activated by Beings that appeared in a dream. I was given a golden-orange liquid to drink that activated my healing abilities and opened up my X-ray vision. In my case, I was given a mini quantum jump in DNA evolution, but I also did my own study to keep pace with those changes. I became a Psychic Surgeon for many years, which also raised my frequency.

Q. *How similar is human DNA to Sasquatch and Mermaids?*

A. Sasquatch is a genetically altered creature. With similar DNA to us, they too are a result of animal and ET experimentation. Some of us carry that genome within us, but not all. Some of us have Angelic coding or other ET coding. There are Angelic beings who took on human form before it was modified and who did not go through the experimentation process mentioned above. Some humans lived in the sea as Mer people. Those who were Mermaids have a DNA memory of it or have a strange longing and love for them.

Even though we could say that we are all of the ocean, we didn't all *live* in the ocean or emerge from the ocean. Our biology contains the *elements* of the ocean in our DNA. Remember, each diverse life form has its unique DNA which has brought about its particular lifeform. Many species have DNA similar to humans, but with unique characteristics which makes them very different from humans.

Q. *Could a spiritual event or severe environmental changes cause a change in DNA?*

A. Yes, both situations can cause shifts in DNA. It is also possible for DNA shifts to occur as varying qualities of light come in from the Cosmos. This could affect life everywhere and cause many changes in activation and adaptation.

Chakras

Aingeal: "Many people have heard of the Chakras through various books or from Eastern traditions. Even though there are many writings on this topic, we thought it would be interesting to bring the subject to Source, who always surprises us with Its view of the things we think we know everything about.

While saying the opening prayer, a beautiful sphere of emerald green light with gold around it appears. Other colors are also emerging—white, red and pink. My initial feeling about these colors is that they relate to the main Chakras of this planet, particularly the emerald green and gold. The emerald green has been the main *planetary* and *personal* Chakra for this particular time period.

Planetarily and as a species, we move through the various Chakra energies through planetary Ages. From the emerald-green Chakra of the Heart we are now moving into the blue Throat Chakra of communication and Truth. Our current planetary shift is taking us into the blue Chakra with the *potential* to reach the violet Chakra of ascension in this time cycle, which is why there is so much focus on love and moving into our hearts.

Emerald green is the color of nurturing, prosperity and love and if we don't incorporate this Ray, we won't be moving into the higher Chakra colors. Green is also the color of Nature, indicating that the plant life and their related Kingdoms have had much to do with upholding this particular Chakra spectrum during this Age.

We began this discussion by sharing information on the Chakras as they relate to planetary Cycles and Ages. The evolution of our species into higher Realms of consciousness is also related to Earth's planetary evolution through these Chakras. The collective mastering of the emerald green Chakra is our current task as a species. We are leaving the Solar-plexus Chakra of power, which deals with our relationship to our own personal power and the Sun. This is why we are seeing so many changes with the Sun. We are in the process of moving from our power center to our heart, which is the emerald green and pink Chakra.

Source is putting a very strong emphasis on Nature. If we destroy Nature, we are not going to make it through to the blue Chakra Cycle.

You can see this process playing out in world affairs: We are in a war between the abuse of power and the correct use of power, which must incorporate the heart to be balanced. This is the task for all of us now—not just in politics and the governments of the world. It is obvious that the resistance from the power abusers is strong. These factions are doing everything they can to stay in their Solar-plexus Chakra in a negative way. Their focus is on taking power away from individuals and using domination and control to suppress free will. Our task as individuals is to come into our own true power, which also connects to our Inner Child through our remembrance of the creative potential and power of our imagination.

Our Inner Child connects us to Source and to our personal purpose. Not only do we need to take back our personal power and lessen our dependency on outer authorities, but we must move from fear into the love of the heart before we can begin to move into the truth and communication with all life that is implicit in the blue Chakra.

Anything that promotes the distortion of power must go, which includes all dogmas and agendas designed to suppress truth, history and the rights of individuals. We need to progress *internally* up the spiritual ladder and understand *true* authority, which is our relationship to our own Inner Sun.

We are moving out of *external* authority and into *internal* authority. This is the main purification process we are in as a planet and as individuals. We are reclaiming our Inner Sun and our Inner Child and releasing our dependence on outer authorities.

The Inner Child is important because it represents the return to the state of harmlessness that can only be found by understanding our own power as creative beings. As long as we believe we are controlled by the outer world, we will not understand ourselves and will not, therefore know our *loving* power. This is why we must return to our Inner Sun before we can ascend and master the emerald green of the Heart. In this purification process there is an emphasis on *forgiveness*— forgiving the past, ourselves, our parents, those who abuse power and anyone who may have injured our self-esteem. In this way, we begin to reclaim our innate Divinity.

Q. *What is a Chakra?*

A. Chakras are appearing as vortex-like spinning cones. Each has a large end that is directed toward our bodies and a smaller end that leads out into various whirlpools to other planes of existence and to other dimensions and realities. Each one seems to be a world in and of itself. Each one is connected to various points in our light bodies and anatomy. They form a network of spiraling vortices that enable interdimensional travel. They can take us to other reality fields for different experiences and when you arrive there, you spend time learning, exploring and having experiences. The Chakras enable you to journey to God Man through learning, experience, knowledge and the attainment of higher frequencies and sounds *as they relate to our Divinity.*

Every system has its own set of Chakras. Our Solar System has a set of main Chakras that lead to different worlds and supply lifeforce energy to our bodies. Spirits come into a particular system to learn about its different dimensional realities as part of its journey to self-realization.

You do not go to another Solar System until you have explored and mastered the varying planets and aspects that relate to the one you're currently in.

When I look at the journey through these different dimensional vortices, I understand that it could take a person a very long time and many lives to travel through these systems, which may explain one of the reasons that we reincarnate. It is not just about the karma we may have created, but it may be more about the mastering of particular Chakras and Solar Systems. Many relationships that people are in focus on mastering particular Chakras. They may incarnate together to work jointly in this way.

I am not talking about the many small Chakras that spiral throughout our anatomy—I am talking about the main Chakras that connect us to other Realms and also feed our anatomy. You could say that the Chakras and the energy that comes through them help create our bodies.

Q. *What are the functions and purposes of Chakras?*

A. The Chakras hold a great ascension potential for self-realization, mastery and experiences of the Universe. They allow us to know God and become God-realized beings. Source is being clear to let us know that our Spirits travel on these vortices of light and sound. The spiraling vortex process that I'm being shown controls how we arrive at particular locations or planes of existence. The vortices provide us the motion and momentum we need to get from one place to the next. This is more of an *inward* process than an outer one.

You may have heard that Chakras break down colors from the Sun and disperse them to our various organs. Each organ in the body vibrates to a particular Chakras and each has its own frequency band of color and sound tone. It isn't only that the Chakras provide colors to the organs; it's that the organs anchor the Chakras to the physical body.

This perspective sheds new light on the subject of organ removal, doesn't it? We all have a 'morphogenetic' (energetic) field that duplicates our physical organs on an etheric level. Source is saying that these energetic counterparts are still intact even if we remove the physical organ relating to it. As long as the energetic template is still intact and not damaged, it still holds its relationship to its associated Chakra.

Q. *Where exactly are the Chakras located?*

A. The Chakras are located throughout our time-space continuum. I'm hearing sound out at those levels. The Chakras *anchor* at different points in the physical body, but they extend quite far out into time-space as well.

Source is asking us to think of ourselves as a tree where the center trunk is going up through the center of our bodies. When you cut a tree and you see the various rings, it indicates the tree's relationship to its own Chakra system. Source is giving us the picture of these rings within rings, or wheels within wheels as a way for us to visualize how the Chakra system looks within us. The difference is that the rings are in a spiraling motion and not stationary.

Chakras don't change location, but they do change their *motion* in that they sometimes rotate clockwise and sometimes counterclockwise, depending upon what's going on in the Cosmos. In other words, if the big gears or wheels in the Universe move in a certain direction, our own Chakras will reverse their spin accordingly to stay in tune with the Universe. These changes in position seem to fluctuate quite frequently. Whether they spin clockwise or counterclockwise or speed up or slow down, is determined by a bigger rotation happening in the Cosmos. Of course, our personal condition can also affect the spin of our Chakras, but there is a larger relationship to our Solar System that we are bringing to light.

Q. *Can we go through the Chakras and describe each one, and where it is anchored in the physical body?*

A. Yes. The red Chakra is anchored two inches below the navel in the lower pelvic region. The orange Chakra is located in the womb/navel area. The yellow Chakra is in the stomach/solar plexus area. The green Chakra encompasses the heart or upper chest area. The blue Chakra covers the throat/thyroid area. The indigo Chakra is in the pituitary or third-eye area in the forehead. The violet Chakra anchors in the pineal gland within the brain. Each Chakra anchors in the body in an area about the size of a half dollar.

When you master a particular Chakra, its color becomes a *Ray*.

Chakras don't remain stationary in a particular location in the body, but actually become vibratory Rays that affect the whole individual when they become a purified essence. For example, we are working on the emerald green of the heart Chakra, purifying it to be able to move into the blue of the throat. On a small level, we see that green is about love and the opening of the heart and blue is about truth and greater communication with all life. However, the bigger picture shows that we are purifying ourselves and our planet to become *Rays of light* that encompass the entire body-mind-spirit system of a person and a planet. This process affects every cell in every part of the body and every cell needs to be vibrating to this emerald green love Ray in order for that Chakra to be incorporated and mastered.

When you move into the blue Chakra, your whole being is in communication with all life everywhere, not just your voice. Mastering particular Chakras involves turning them into Rays that *become* your physiology and your very essence. Once Earth has harmonized the green Ray and moved into the blue Ray, its primary color will be blue.

The smaller Chakra wheels in the body are anchoring points that nourish the body at particular body locations or organ sites. The bigger Chakra mastery however, is all encompassing.

When I talk about the emerald green/love that we're working on now, there may be people who do not complete the mastery of this Chakra this time around. Keep in mind that we first have to reverse where we place our power from external to internal in the solar-plexus Chakra before the emerald green Chakra of the heart can be mastered. We need these two Chakras purified and turned into Rays within us before we can move into the blue. You can see that this time period that we are in offers us an accelerated opportunity for rapid transformation.

If we do not master these opportunities now, Source is telling us not to worry because there will be many opportunities to cycle through these Chakras again and again. Ultimately, we will all make it. Time and attention are only focal points in a lifetime, so don't be hard on yourself if you feel you still have issues to resolve. Do your best. If it is your desire for purification however, this is the time to do it at a fast pace. We are being given much aid from various sources to help us heal and progress.

Q. *Why do we need Chakras at all?*

A. The Chakras are part of the design of our particular Solar System. They are our ladder of ascent, allowing us to be connected and evolve to God Man. You need them to become God Man in this dimension. They are energetic templates, or 'maps', for our biology in this Universe. As you come down through the levels, these templates hold certain geometries in place. When we get close to God Realization, they disappear from the light body and the physical body and you are able to move out of this Solar System. You become a Flame of Source. While you are in your awakening process however, the Chakra system is your key to becoming whole in this dimension. It holds the geometries that allow expansion to happen. They are part of the ladder the Kundalini uses as it spirals up the body.

Q. *Why are there sound tones connected to the Chakras?*

A. I see spinning, spiraling cones that extend way out into time-space and connect into our physical bodies. Sound is the vibration that is necessary for the making of and dissolution of matter and the ascension into light. It is the vibratory action or *motion* of creation. Each Chakra has a particular sound that matches its plane of existence. It's something that needs to be heard from within. It is an *internal traveling* system. I say 'internal', but the traveling can occur internally and externally.

There is the notion in some teachings that each Chakra vibrates to a particular note on the harmonic scale. However, the inner transformation that accompanies a particular Chakra or plane of existence has its own particular sound tone frequency. The sound can't be described—it can only be experienced. I'm hearing those tones now, but I can't describe them to you because they are my personal, inner experience. I can hear the Chakras hum and sing. Each will be heard internally by the individual when he/she is ready. If you are incorporating a Chakra into yourself, you will hear the sound tones and you'll see the colors and virtuous symbols associated with the particular Chakra.

Q. *Why is it important for us as humans to go through these particular Chakras? Why do we have to master these planes of existence in our particular sphere of reality?*

A. Source is saying it's because we don't get out of a particular system until we master its planes of existence. We can't move into a different Universe until we cycle through and master or incorporate within us, the planes of existence in our particular Solar System. It has to do with the frequency we are currently resonating to. Each Solar System has its own series of frequency ranges that create the life forms in its varying dimensions. The life forms in a Solar System have to evolve through the various frequencies until they are ready to go beyond that system into another set of frequencies.

It is part of becoming God-realized because God Realization means that you *become* everything. We continue to reincarnate until we become an Ascended Master of our particular system. Only then are we free to move out of it. Being an Ascended Master of a system means that you are an Ascended Master of *that particular system*, but not of the entire Universe. You will have mastered or gained the qualities and abilities inherent in that particular system. This mastering is actually a desire of the Individuated Spirit/soul as it journeys through the Universe and becomes a co-creator with it.

Q. *What do the Chakras have to do with our biology and its relationship to enlightenment?*

A. The Chakras were designed to feed us sunlight and color while we're in a body. Their swirling forcefields helped create the body. Human biology was created so we could learn about different dimensions within a system and be a life contributor to that system. A Sun is designed to feed the lifeforms of a particular system and give them exactly what they need to survive while in that system. We were designed to live off sunlight, as it is a complete menu of colors, sound tones and frequencies for our biology. We began to consume other life forms—meats, plants and fruits as a result of externalizing our consciousness and digressing our biology through history.

We have been talking about an *inner* journey and earlier we talked about Kundalini, which is also an inner journey that uses the Chakra system. Now we are talking about the Chakras having dual functions. One function is to break down sunlight and disperse those color rays to the various organs in our bodies to feed us while we're in a physical body.

The other function is to expand our consciousness and mastery of this system through the different dimensional levels of existence in our Solar System so that we may become God-realized.

However, once we became externalized in our *consciousness*, we forgot our inward journey to God Realization and began to focus only on our individualized body or alter-ego presence. We got caught up in what was manifesting in our reality externally so that our focus of attention became material rather than spiritual. We forgot that manifestation occurs from within to without. We forgot how to live off of sunlight and we began to consume other lifeforms for energy. When you become a true mystic, or someone who is devoted to their inner path, you move through the various planes of existence and dimensional levels and begin to hear the inner sound tones associated with your Chakra system. Soon you lose your interest in consuming outer life forms and as you move up into higher frequencies, you will *naturally* move once again toward living on sunlight and eventually not even need that. You can begin to see the change in yourself as you move away from eating denser foods to lighter foods, to more liquids, to sunlight, to becoming a *source* of spiritual sustenance yourself. As you become more God Man, you become a Sun that *radiates* lifeforce rather than *takes* lifeforce.

In the consumption of foods, we are not saying that eating meat is low consciousness or that becoming a vegetarian or a raw food vegan is the optimal way to be. You could have a cow whose meat is filled with high quality color and sound as much as a plant could be filled with environmental toxins. You have to trust and follow your own particular intuition and biological requirements until you *naturally* evolve past consuming other life forms. The word *naturally* is key here because unless it is a natural progression to move to lighter forms of food and then to sunlight, you will become ill or starve. Only when you have reached the frequency of incorporating more spirit will it be safe for you to adjust the way you receive lifeforce energy.

I recently got a message from an old yogi who told me to eat only *happy* foods, which, as we mentioned previously, are foods you tune into while grocery shopping that feel happy to you. There were no specific types of foods mentioned, except for consuming more edible flowers.

'Happy foods' could be a particular piece of meat you notice, or a raw food or a canned vegetable. You get the point. Shopping for happy foods is an *intuitive* exercise; what you are drawn to will change with every shopping adventure.

Q. *Can we consciously control our Chakras to heal our bodies?*

A. Source is asking us, "What would you do with them?" It implies that unless you have a full understanding of a Chakra and what it's connected to on every level—physical, mental, emotional and spiritual all the way out into the different dimensional levels and planes of existence, you won't fully understand its qualities or potentials. You can focus all the attention you want on a Chakra, thinking you're clearing and balancing it, but you could be doing so with inadequate information. For example, many healers have the idea that a Chakra should only spin clockwise, and if they see a Chakra in their client spinning counterclockwise, they will reverse its spin, not realizing that sometimes Chakra spin clockwise and sometimes counterclockwise as part of their alignment with Cosmic energies. It is an in-breath and out-breath.

Meditating on the Chakras helps us gather their information and *know* them. As we now know, Chakras lead to new worlds and realities yet to be discovered. Source is saying that if you want to work with Chakras for healing, the way to do it is to know them deeply on an internal level first, so that it can be integrated fully within your biology. This is what causes true healing and transformation. You can work with colors in a therapeutic way to either add colors to the body where there is a deficiency or take away color where there is excess. Much healing can be done with the color and sound levels of our biology. Those levels are a small part of healing in the context of our expansion, but anything that brings more balance and awareness is helpful.

Q. *Can putting Reiki on a Chakra help increase wealth?*

A. True prosperity is coming to the place where you love yourself and all life unconditionally. You come to the place where you no longer have any judgments, fears or harmful intent toward anything or anyone; this puts you in the flow of life and love where you are sustained by this in your everyday life. Prosperity has to do with coming into wholeness and recognizing you are not a separate entity, but are in a flowing relationship with all life everywhere. The corresponding harmlessness that goes along with this realization naturally provides prosperity.

So, I'm not getting a "yes" to this question regarding Reiki and prosperity because prosperity is not just associated with the Chakras. True prosperity is about becoming the abundance of the Universe within yourself.

To have prosperity at the level of which you are asking, the task at hand is to undo fear, which is the underlying issue under all experiences of apparent lack. Fear stops the flow of the natural life currents that provide for us. Whether you're in the flow or out of it is really the issue. Fear blocks the flow of natural good in our lives. This is where Reiki can be of benefit—it supplies people with a higher frequency of lifeforce energy, enabling them to release fear and heal.

Q. *Is psychic ability related to healing the Chakras?*

A. You will gain more of these abilities as you incorporate the qualities and attributes of the Chakras and Kundalini currents within yourself. As you go into your inner temple and gain more knowledge of yourself and your Chakras, the gifts associated with each Chakra will become active as part of your natural state. These gifts are built into your biology and are waiting to be activated. These gifts are enormous. They are not limited to psychic ability, but incorporate tremendous regenerative abilities as well as the heightening of all our senses.

Your *natural* abilities already include bilocation, teleportation, dematerialization, interdimensional movement and meeting other aspects of yourself in other dimensions and planes of existence. The ability to smell and taste someone from miles away is also part of our natural gifts. This ability has a high level of discernment connected to it, allowing us to know the quality and frequency of various life forms before we come upon them physically. Working with the Chakras and Kundalini will go a long way toward bringing forth and activating these gifts within us.

Q. *What can we do to activate or enhance these abilities?*

A. Besides what we have already mentioned, you can begin *Sun gazing*, which is centering and regenerative. Practiced with caution, it can strengthen your inner core and activate higher abilities. Start gazing at the Sun for 1-2 seconds in the morning as the Sun is rising and again 1-2 seconds when the Sun is setting. Keeping safety in mind, you increase by a few seconds each day. Information online will show you the rest of the practice and how to *safely* increase the time spent gazing at the Sun.

Meditate on your Chakras and begin *journaling*. Question your beliefs, thoughts, feelings and intentions. Change your diet if it is unhealthy, so that your entire system can function better. The quality of your food determines its nutritional value for you. Food affects your energy levels, your moods and even your thoughts. Amino acids, minerals and vitamins and 'happy foods' are the basics to a healthy system.

You have a Guardian Angel assisting you in your evolution. This indwelling Holy Spirit will help you on your journey, if that is your intention. Take some time to explore and focus daily on these parts of you. Even 15 minutes of quiet inner focus and smiling at your organs and spirit will begin to awaken and create an inner relationship with your system.

When you meditate, call on this Holy Spirit within you and ask it to teach you. Ask it to give you the knowledge you need at this time. You can ask your Guardian Angel to show you which Chakra needs attention or has some virtue or knowledge to impart to you. Be patient with yourself and wait for an answer.

Answers can take many forms—anything from hearing an answer inside yourself or receiving a feeling of peace or direct knowing. Your answer may come through a phone call or an event that happens. You may begin to receive impressions of colors that have feelings or information connected to them. A symbol may appear that you have to look up to discover its meaning. You may come upon a book or document that speaks directly to you and answers your questions.

There are many ways that answers can be delivered. The more practice you give it, the more proficient you become at discovering your Inner Self. Make it a daily practice if possible, because the more attention you put on focusing within, the more the glands associated with your higher gifts become activated.

Q. *Are humans the only ones with Chakras?*

A. Humans, animals, plants, even rocks have Chakras. Every life form has a Chakra system at the level of its own design. Remember, Chakras are the way life forms are connected to the Cosmos and are how sunlight breaks down and feeds bodies.

Q. *Can Chakras be damaged?*

A. Yes. For example, if you have a wound or injury, it can damage the Chakra that's connected to it. Chakras can also be stolen by negative entities. You can have missing Chakras. Food can affect the health of the biology and its Chakra system. Your environment also plays a part. The Chakras are designed to nourish you, but if your template is disturbed or out of balance in some way it will affect the health of the Chakra and the corresponding organs.

Chakras are affected by many things, including traumas from this life or past lives as well as biological disturbances. This is another reason why we suggest you go within and learn about your own Chakras and see their condition, so you can make adjustments or healing where necessary. Your Holy Spirit within will show you what to do. Your Holy Spirit is your Higher Mind and the part that remembers God. You may also find that you are suddenly attracted to a particular healer who may have the tools to provide healing for you.

Q. *Are specific diseases or sicknesses related to each Chakra?*

A. I am being guided to address the *Feet* Chakras first, even though they're not considered one of the main Chakras. The Feet Chakras are in the middle of each foot and go from the top of the foot through to the bottom of the foot. These Chakras connect you to the Earth grid. The energy coming up from the Earth grid through these Chakra points can either be health producing or sickness producing, depending upon your location. The first thing to look at when we are checking Chakras is what's coming up from the Earth in your area. This is important now because there are so many Earth changes occurring, especially at the level of the electromagnetic field/grids of the Earth. We need to see if we're standing on healthy or toxic grids. Grids fluctuate, but they don't fluctuate to a huge degree minute-by-minute unless there is earthquake activity or some other catalyst such as solar flares, volcanic activity or methane gas buildup beneath the surface. The exception to these is unnatural stimulation of land areas by fracking, drilling or government/military subsurface programs or projects. Grids can also become toxic from polluted water, compromised vortices, traumas related to historical events or graveyards that have been disturbed.

Living on toxic grids or geopathic stress points will affect your health and balanced perception because they affect equilibrium on all levels. They affect your mental and emotional state as well as the functioning of your nervous system.

The *Root* Chakra, which is below the navel, is concerned with what we inherit from our parents. This is the Chakra where conception occurs. In the sexual exchange between our mother and father, their genetic ancestry, their gifts and issues get transferred to the newly emerging fetus and become part of it's anatomy. The Root Chakra also holds our connection to our other lives. This is where we bring forward not only what we've inherited from our parents, but also our own soul history from other lives. The information stored in this Chakra can affect the organs related to this Chakra and can also manifest as issues that would be connected to this Chakra.

Keep in mind that we may be inheriting fabulous things from our ancestry and other lives, but we may also be inheriting some of our parent's unhealed issues as well as our own from other lifetimes. If we *do* inherit some negative patterns, it could take the form of illnesses in that area of our body, or we could attract particular experiences or patterns to ourselves that would connect to that area of our body. We may also *not* manifest any aberration in that Chakra! Since this Chakra connects to sexuality, pleasure, pain and the creation of life forms, we may want to see how these are evidencing themselves in our own lives.

The *Navel* Chakra, which is in the area of the bellybutton or navel, is the Chakra that begins to *anchor* us into the physical world. The Root Chakra controls what we inherit, and the Navel Chakra controls the process of *anchoring* what we inherit into our body and the planet. There is a particular harmonic in the Naval Chakra that needs to be developed correctly from the beginning. This Chakra makes sure we are anchored correctly in this particular dimension. Distortions in any of these Chakras can manifest as illnesses or issues pertaining to those Chakras, but they won't necessarily manifest specifically in those areas.

The *Solar Plexus* Chakra has to do with our relationship to the Sun and Moon. It is important to look at what the Sun and Moon were doing when you were born or when you were conceived.

If you are lucky enough to have an aware mother, it would be worth having a talk with her about the timing of your conception. It is also possible to remember your conception through Rebirthing or Past Life Regression, which is where Astrology can be of good use. The position of the Sun and Moon and their activities during the time of your birth and conception get anchored in your biology. Understanding this can help you get clear on the benefits and influences that could show up as patterns in your life.

The *Heart* Chakra, located in the area of the heart, ironically holds our fear of death. I find this quite interesting because until we get through the fear of death and overcome death in our consciousness, we cannot know true Love. As long as we have fear, our ability to love and surrender to our oneness with life will be thwarted. Fear keeps us in a separatist perception concerned only with self-preservation at the expense of the whole. We can see how this relates to what is going on in the world today. It is obvious when we are talking about these Chakras that if the distortions we inherit are not cleared or healed, it affects us throughout time on many levels.

The *Throat* Chakra, located at the throat area, is about manifesting through sound. Long ago, we didn't have words as we do now. We emitted specific sound tones from our throat area that were designed to cause deliberate manifestations. The sound tone frequencies were very pure and would produce instant manifestations. I am seeing mouths that are open and look like they have a circular, open shape as the sound tones are being emitted. These are sound tone *calls* that are not words. Sound is what brings things into matter and also disassembles matter. If we could recapture this original ability and emit these sound tones in their pure frequency, we could heal just about anything. We could build up or tear down as required. The ancient time I am tuning into was before we became this dense in matter. We were not solely spirit beings; we did have form, but it wasn't as dense as ours is now. We did not have language, but only sound tones.

The *Third Eye* Chakra, located at the pituitary gland in the center of the forehead, sets our *horizontal* axis and frame of reference. I see a horizontal ray of light coming out of that Chakra that affects our *linear* reality—how and what we see and perceive. Our ability to see and perceive in this dimension is very limited at this point because this Chakra is not fully activated in most of us. If it were, we would see and notice many more things in our field of vision than we do now. We would also be seeing the multidimensional levels that exist here, right now. In this Chakra, we are predominantly concerned with *sight* and our horizontal orientation in this dimension. However, there is a point in the evolution of this Chakra up the ladder of ascent where our visual orientation changes and disconnects from the physical.

The *Crown* Chakra at the top of the head, has to do with our *vertical* axis. Energy comes down through the top of our head and down to Earth to set our vertical orientation in time and space. We have a set of geometries within us that need this axis to be able to rotate and spin.

The vertical axis allows our sacred geometries to spin so that our core template stays in order. I feel a lot of heat while I'm exploring this Chakra from the top to bottom in my body. This Chakra puts us in touch with the Christ Mind and allows us to anchor this Mind and knowledge into the physical world. It can change the body entirely. It can regenerate cells, change biology, bring in more light and electricity into the system and connect us to cosmic consciousness while being anchored in the physical body. It can also de-anchor us from the physical body. This Chakra is your key to flight.

Kundalini

Aingeal: "In this section we asked Source about Kundalini, which many mystical systems describe as the serpent fire located at the base of each person's spine. It is notable that as I was saying the opening prayer, a burst of brilliant pure white light entered the room. As I was tapering off with the prayer, streaks of yellow and royal blue penetrated through the white light."

Q. *What is Source's definition of Kundalini?*

A. Source defines Kundalini as *The Path of Courage*—specifically, the courage to become our True Self as we were created. The journey to our True Self is not easily achieved—rather, it is something that requires challenges and victories along the way. Conceptually, we have been taught that our True Self is something that is already perfect and whole in God, but what I hear Source saying is that to *become* or *actualize* your True Self *as you were created*, is a courageous effort and journey. Kundalini is an essential part of this journey.

Kundalini is the ladder of ascension that was put in our bodies. It is dormant in its capabilities to the un-awakened. It is the *potential* for God Realization that is locked inside our bodies and certain keys are required to open it. Those keys are related to the journey and are therefore related to courage, perseverance, sincerity, honor and other high virtues. The development of virtues is a requirement for God Realization. If you try to activate Kundalini without the corresponding virtues on the ladder of ascent, you can become ill or cause distortions and imbalances because Kundalini is a purifying fire.

Kundalini *arrives* at radiance—the burst of white light I saw at the beginning of this session. It arrives at this radiance when it is purified and refined. Adepts on the journey *become* this radiance once they have purified themselves and become the embodiment of higher virtues. Symbols associated with this accomplishment are the Thousand-Petal Lotus, the Sun, the Diamond, the Swan, the White Rose and the Flame, to name a few.

You may have read about adepts in the past who achieved God Realization. They are described as wearing a white raiment, indicating the white light they have become and are now *sources* of God radiance. This white light is a powerful force similar to white fire—it is dynamic in its activity and expansiveness. It is not a sweet, ineffective white light, but rather a powerful, purified force of Creation, which is also pure Love.

Kundalini needs to spiral around and through the Chakras in order to open up certain keys. There is an order to the spiraling process and each key along its path in the body has its own corresponding virtues. Kundalini is a raw fire or electrical current that we hold as a regenerative *potential* in our bodies. It is unrefined in its raw state. This is important because unrefined Kundalini can manifest itself as vices. In other words, if that energy or sacred fire is not purified and does not become virtuous, it can remain a force that causes destruction or turns in on itself.

Source is calling Kundalini, *The Path of Courage* because the bringing forth of the divine presence in Kundalini is an honorable and challenging journey of purification that results in the transformation of our lower animal nature to our higher God Man. The animal/reptilian nature is what requires purification. It is the part of us that is warlike, aggressive, controlling, dominating, greedy, selfish and murderous. It is also judgmental and destructive. We will not get rid of this part of ourselves entirely because it supports our survival instinct, but this portion of us needs to be lessened by developing our higher nature and higher brain.

Q. *Do we have conscious control over the growth of courage?*

A. Source is saying "Yes and No". There are times when the conditions inside a person can cause Kundalini to spontaneously arise, seemingly out of nowhere. It could be that a person isn't necessarily aware on their path and suddenly this force arises within them as a predetermined event. In other words, the *soul* would have arranged for this to occur at a specific time based on its prior experiences and soul contract.

Here's an example: Let's say that you had things you didn't finish in a particular past life. It could be that you didn't master some things in physical life. You may have come back in this life to master those things. You could be operating very much in the mundane 3D world, then suddenly one day, you experience Kundalini rising. This would be a predetermined event giving you time to master your physical issues in the 3D world before you take on the continued journey of ascent up the ladder. Kundalini rising changes a person's entire orientation in 3D.

As for consciously controlling the development of Kundalini, you can use certain disciplines to activate the Kundalini but you need to be ready to take on the challenges and courage needed for the ensuing purification process. As the Kundalini rises, it spirals up through your Chakras and causes them to move or spin in their rotation. Each Chakra has its own unique vice to be purified, so that its higher virtue can be attained, much as a diamond in the rough needs to be refined to bring out its brilliance. So, if you're going to consciously discipline yourself through various techniques to raise your Kundalini, you need to be ready for this purification process so that the Kundalini currents can perform in the way they were meant to perform on the path to becoming God Man.

If you've been on the spiritual path and have not been aware of this Kundalini process but you have been clearing your lower self through other means, your Kundalini currents may have been slowly rising through this process without you consciously being aware of it.

In other words, if you have been achieving virtues by going through various challenges in your life and making higher choices, chances are your Kundalini has been rising slowly as you perfect yourself. It would be doing this very gently and naturally, as opposed to a huge rush that someone who is experiencing spontaneous Kundalini rising might experience.

If you have been raising your Kundalini gently and naturally, you will have noticed specific results such as an increase in psychic ability, heightened senses, deeper communication with all life, more compassion, harmless intent toward everyone and everything, an increase in sensitivity, a greater ability to be aware of things at subtler levels, increased telepathy and many other higher gifts. You will also be having continual experiences of greater and greater all-encompassing Love.

You may also find that others are naturally awakened or healed in your presence. You may find yourself taking journeys out of your body, teleporting or bi-locating, meeting other selves in other dimensions or communicating with spirit beings from other dimensions or the elemental kingdom.

Q. *Does Kundalini start from the base of the spine, the base Chakra, the core of the Earth or somewhere else?*

A. It does *not* come from Earth's core. It is part of our body's spinal-cord system. The spinal column is our ladder of ascent. It has Chakra points on it that are portals where the Kundalini currents can rise and spiral. I feel that I'm in the lower back when I'm looking for Kundalini's origin. Source is saying that it originates in the Primal Self. In most of us Kundalini is dormant. We can call it our own potentized lifeforce energy that allows us to be regenerated when activated. It is part of our biology and part of the workings of our Central Nervous System in the central column of the spine. Another name for this central column is the *Pranic Tube*.

Q. *Does Kundalini connect us to other planets or universes?*

A. Source is saying "No". The question is a bit of a distraction in that it will take you away from the journey of Kundalini as a Path of Courage. When you reach the state of actualizing yourself as white light, you achieve freedom. Once that happens, you are in communication or at one with all life and this then encompasses other planets and universes.

Q. *Is Kundalini a natural part of all other life forms?*

A. Not in the potential that we are speaking today. Animals, for example, have some of this lifeforce energy within them, but it remains confined to their instinctual nature. Animals cannot consciously work with this energy as humans can. In other words, animals are not taking on the Path of Courage. It is predominantly humans on this planet that can actualize themselves as God Men and become white light beings. Animals do not have the DNA capability to consciously ascend through decision-making and attaining virtues. The same is true of plants or minerals. However, our evolution does affect all life forms on this planet and catalyzes them to a more evolved state.

Q. *Do aliens experience Kundalini?*

A. Yes, they do in their own degrees. One of the things Source wants us to know is that there are alien species that are *beneath* humans in their evolutionary process. Therefore, not every alien species has the same potential. Not every alien species has the same Kundalini capability that we are speaking of today. Yet, there are some alien species that have gone far beyond Earth humans in potentiality and actuality.

Q. *Can we stimulate Kundalini awakening artificially?*

A. 'Artificially' is a loaded word. We are assuming that you mean through the use of hallucinogens or various other techniques. The use of these things can stimulate Kundalini currents to rise, but Source is saying that if you want to become an actualized God being, you have to do the Path of Courage to become virtuous. You can artificially stimulate Kundalini currents and have visionary experiences through artificial stimulants, which may provide you a glimpse of life at deeper spiritual levels, but the process of actually *becoming* God Man is something that is a purification process from the lower nature to the higher nature. If you're going to stimulate Kundalini currents in artificial ways, be prepared to do the purification work that will show up as you rise up the ladder of ascent through the Chakra system. Only through this process do you actually integrate and become a being of radiant light.

Q. *Can Kundalini rising cause physical or mental damage?*

A. Yes, it can if you cannot handle the purification required at the various levels of ascent. Kundalini will not only activate many higher gifts, but it will alter your perception of reality. Imagine having your orientation of the world being completely turned around, and while that is happening, all of your suppressed emotions and thoughts begin to surface. Everything will change and clearing and integrating these changes is a huge undertaking. We are talking about uprooting beliefs about the world, yourself and God that you may have brought with you through many lifetimes as well as clearing any unhealed trauma you may still be carrying from this life or others.

If you activate the Kundalini at a time when you're not really ready to take on this path, it can cause damage on many levels. Kundalini is similar to being struck by lightning. Some people die when struck by lightning, others suffer physical bodily damage, while others have illuminating visionary experiences of God or other worlds.

Those who survive such an experience will come back changed, but they may need years of rehabilitation to recover from the physical damage. A Kundalini experience greatly affects your nervous system and biology and its force changes nerve centers as it goes up the spine. It produces an entire new physiology. We need to understand that the nervous system within each person is a delicate and sensitive system, so make sure that you are ready and honoring that sensitivity if you choose to artificially stimulate the rising of your Kundalini.

Q. *Would someone who has never heard of Kundalini or never had any exposure to it experience Kundalini just like a person who knows about it?*

A. What I'm hearing from Source is that there would have been some previous buildup or knowledge about Kundalini in the person from other lives. Even if a person comes into this life with no recollection of past lives, or never having heard of Kundalini in this life, it is most likely that they would have had knowledge or experience of it at some point in a past life. Their soul would know what they had been doing in this area prior to this incarnation. I'm not seeing that someone would have a spontaneous Kundalini rising without some prior experience from another time.

Q. *Is Kundalini a necessary part of life or death? Is its rising something we are trying to achieve during this lifetime? Is Kundalini a prerequisite to a new incarnation?*

A. There are actually many things that stimulate a new incarnation. There is so much to life, people and their experiences; there are many things people reincarnate for. They come back to resolve issues, to forgive, to play and have fun.

Some come back for revenge, others come back to continue their path of ascent. Others may come back just to have a family or experience a particular occupation. All of these things are stages or steps along the way to becoming enlightened. Your awakening and that of your Kundalini are natural processes.

The Path of Courage has a sequence to it: If someone has a spontaneous Kundalini rising, you can expect there was a past life history where they would have built up a sequence of events that would arrive at the rising. When a person gets ready to become God actualized, Kundalini rising is a deep event inside of them that is a natural result of prior transformative work.

There are those who come into their lives naturally seeking knowledge or exhibiting mature wisdom at very young ages, which indicates prior lives of maturing.

Kundalini is not a prerequisite to a new incarnation—it is the God force that *accompanies* a new incarnation. It is a necessary part of life because it allows the body functions to occur. At its most primal nature, it is the force for survival and reproduction of the species. At its highest nature, it allows us the evolution into God Man. It isn't a factor in the death process.

Q. *Does where you live, where you've been, or what's happening on the planet affect the rising of Kundalini?*

A. There are power spots on Earth where the frequency is high enough to stimulate awakenings. While I don't see them giving you a full Kundalini rising, they wouldn't thwart it either.

What's happening on the planet can affect the rising of Kundalini, depending upon the cosmic forces in play. At some level, we all expect to be stimulated by these forces. Light codes from the Cosmos can affect the biology of species. Light codes can stimulate human DNA and cause varying degrees of Kundalini awakening. You could say we all share a collective agreement to be here for Kundalini awakening to the degree that we are each ready for it.

Let's look at places, not from the point of Kundalini rising, but rather from the viewpoint of *nourishment*. Different land areas have different qualities and frequencies. Some places work well for certain people who get nourished and stimulated by the energies there, while other places deplete a person's nourishment. One needs to evaluate places individually, as one place may help one person but hurt another. Places that are right for you should make you feel good, supported and happy. You should feel healthier and happier when you're in the right place.

There is an exception to this, however, in that you can be in a place that feels very nourishing to you and still go through challenges that would be designed to push you further or make you grow beyond your current limits. In these cases, the place would still be considered good for you. There is discernment needed because a place that is unhealthy for you may not give you challenges that make you stretch your limits, but rather drain your energy and take you down. Those types of challenges are unhealthy. The question becomes 'When are challenges good for you and when are they destructive to your growth?' This is how you evaluate if where you are is the best place for you. So, where you are does not necessarily determine whether or not your Kundalini will rise.

Q. *Can we facilitate Kundalini awakening by diet or exercise?*

A. Changing your diet and exercising can be part of the purification process by making sure that your cells are in the best condition possible to handle and integrate the higher frequency of Kundalini rising. However, these changes alone will not accomplish the *virtues* necessary to integrate Kundalini, because becoming God Man—actualizing that within your biology and consciousness—requires the attainment of virtues.

Cleansing the body and keeping it in a state of vitality can help your nervous system and organs handle the Kundalini energy and use it for regeneration.

If your body is in a state of ill health because of your diet or lack of fitness, chances are the Kundalini energy will not be able to flow properly through your various channels as easily as it could if you were in a better state of nourishment and vitality. These things are part of the *process*. There are many breathing techniques that help stimulate Kundalini energy. Many of these techniques also bring up unhealed issues out of the cells for cleansing, which is another type of purification process. Rebirthing and Transformational Breathing are some examples of techniques that help facilitate this cleansing process.

Q. *I fell off a horse and landed on my tailbone sending a shock up my spine. Can spinal injuries cause or stop a Kundalini rising?*

A. Injuries can either interfere with Kundalini currents or activate them. Traumas can block the flow of those currents if the injuries have affected your spinal cord or nervous system. However, if you are *consciously* taking on the journey of moving the Kundalini, there are many things you can do to remove blockages. Even though Kundalini is connected naturally to the body, it can also move up the light bodies. You may have heard we all have what's called a 'morphogenetic field', which is an exact duplicate of our physical organs but is in our energy body and is invisible to us.

This field is why people who have lost a physical organ or limb still say they feel as if the organ or limb is still there. You can move Kundalini spiritually through the morphogenetic field or through other lightbody channels, which could happen as a result of doing clearing work or by consciously moving your Kundalini energy. In other words, you can bypass the physical vehicle and still achieve Kundalini awakening.

Kundalini has regenerative as well as destructive abilities, depending upon what it encounters in your biology along the way. Remember, the attainment of virtues contains healing properties because all virtues are expressions of Love.

The Path of Courage is really the path of the mystic, because you become aware of deeper and deeper levels of Love and compassion. As you become illuminated in your consciousness, your physical body can be affected in positive ways.

Q. *Can Kundalini rising happen at any age?*

A. Source is saying it can, but it's unlikely that it would. Children are being born these days with varying degrees of activation and some already have a certain degree of Kundalini integration put in place within their biology. For normal children, it's unlikely that Kundalini would spontaneously arise fully because their biology and consciousness is too unrefined and underdeveloped. However, it has been said that a normal Kundalini awakening process occurs at ages 11, 22, 33 and 44. However, it is questionable whether our current DNA strands are working properly for this natural process to occur.

Storms in Nature exhibit incredible power and force and we can consider that Kundalini energy is a force of this magnitude within our physical body. Its potential is unlimited, which is why Kundalini raising should be done with conscious maturity.

We are dealing with the literal God force that has been put into our biology as a safeguard—not only for our survival, but for our resurrection and ascension into a God Realized being. If we could truly understand the sacredness of it, we would treat our physical bodies with more respect. We could say that Kundalini is our savior in that it can get us out of the death cycle we have been in for millennia.

Many people have varying degrees of Kundalini awakening but few understand what it really means to become a blaze of pure white fire. To actualize it and *become* the God force, to radiate it, is a sacred event. It is an event of pure, dynamic Love. This force can transmute your body into light. You can see that this path involves great maturity and responsibility.

Many of us have ideas or desires to become Godlike, but few of us understand the responsibility and the purification of the lower self that is necessary to actualize this potential within ourselves, which is why Source is calling it the *Path of Courage*.

Q. *Is the sex act connected to Kundalini energy?*

A. The sex act and drive is an *aspect* of Kundalini energy, especially when it is activated by Love. In one way, Kundalini is the force that allows reproduction to occur—it is the lifeforce current that enables us to bring forth a new life form. It ensures the survival of the species. Kundalini rising can be stimulated through sexual exchange and higher love between people and there are various methods like Tantric sex that focus on raising the Kundalini through sexual exchange. This type of Kundalini rising can be just as valuable as any other that stimulates Kundalini.

The important thing to remember is that Kundalini is an alchemical force that is not meant to stay in the lower Chakras, but rather is meant to rise up the Chakra system into the brain, producing enlightenment and Divine Love at its highest level. The ancient Egyptians also used sexual rituals to cause Kundalini to rise and they deliberately used sexual encounters to promote inner enlightenment. It is not necessary to have sexual encounters or rituals to raise Kundalini, however. The sex act is one way. Your own inner journey also activates Kundalini.

* * *

Q. *Can hallucinogens or ayahuasca affect Kundalini?*

A. You have to be able to handle the effects of these drug experiences. Some people can have a spiritual vision or an experience of unity where they feel they are becoming one with Mother Earth. The aftereffects of any kind of brain opening still requires purification and integration of the lower levels of one's anatomy. The physical body needs to be able to integrate the chemicals that are released during a drug related experience.

If the physical body is unable to handle this shift, these experiences can damage the lower centers, which is why people who have excessive drug experiences can become unbalanced in their everyday lives. This is also why Source advises us to work with Kundalini in a sacred way, understanding that it is a ladder of ascent up through the Chakra system that purifies the alter-ego so that the entire body can hold and attain its higher nature. People cannot benefit from experiencing unity or Love if they are unable to integrate the experience into their own biology and everyday life. Source looks at Kundalini as an incredibly sacred and powerful ladder to God Realization, which is why caution is advised if you are going to artificially stimulate Kundalini energy through hallucinogens.

Q. *Describe how Kundalini Yoga helps the body and soul?*

A. Kundalini Yoga can be very purifying if it is done consciously and with breathwork, allowing you to be very aware of the energy as it travels up your spine. Because this type of yoga is a conscious process, its practitioner also becomes aware of issues that may arise for purification and thus is better able to deal with them than someone who is less conscious. Kundalini Yoga can be very healing and purifying if it is done correctly and it can help heal the body and also progress the Individuated Spirit, which builds the soul energy.

Q. *What are the jolts, or krias, that occur during meditation?*

A. Jolts are evidence of Kundalini becoming active within the body. Other people may call these experiences *activations;* they can be considered minor Kundalini awakenings.

Q. *What happens to the Kundalini energy when we die?*

A. Source is saying it goes with the Spirit of the person when they die. It moves out of the body at death, bringing the Spirit into the white-light experience. What an incredible failsafe!

We are given a failsafe, no matter what circumstance or level of consciousness we find ourselves in. You have the powers of basic reproduction and the ability to expand your consciousness in unlimited ways. You have the ability to overcome death, and if you don't overcome death, your Kundalini goes back through the tunnel into the spirit planes. The Kundalini also has healing and regenerative powers while in the physical body. It can change your body chemistry and make you an eternal life being, whether physical or in spirit. Kundalini is your God force within, so we can take the phrase 'God is Within' quite literally.

When we die, the Kundalini acts like an arrow that propels us back into the spirit planes, which is a different process then when someone becomes an actualized God being while in the physical body. The Kundalini will take you back no matter what level of consciousness you have achieved in a given lifetime. Once you become a God being however, you *yourself* will decide whether you turn yourself into spirit or light or stay in a physical body indefinitely. In other words, when you are God Realized, death has no authority over you.

Q. *Is Kundalini our indwelling God spirit?*

A. Yes! You've got it! Kundalini is your God spirit contained within your body! You can now see how we incarnate, bringing a portion of our Spirit with us. It lies dormant at the base of our spine, allowing us to live and be alive in this dimension. It allows us the powers of reproduction, but it also has the ability to turn us into God made flesh once it is awakened. You can now also see how the Path of Courage is a journey we take as spirit beings to the awakening of our own God within.

Kundalini is our Spirit in the body. Our Spirit grows and develops into maturity and mastery through the purification of the lower, or animal nature. If we stay asleep in our consciousness, our Kundalini will also remain dormant providing our basic survival functions. As our consciousness awakens to the truth of who we are, our Kundalini also awakens.

This was a great question and if it hadn't been asked, we would have missed this realization. Now, when we read over this chapter, we may look at these answers in a very different light.

Q. Once, by accident, I had a spontaneous Kundalini experience during an acupuncture treatment. After that, the acupuncturist would not use those same points. Did the practitioner restrain my Kundalini's rising, or did he facilitate its rising in some way?

A. First, there are no accidents. Some part of you would have known that your Kundalini was going to be activated by going to this practitioner. So ask yourself, what has been the effects for you of that Kundalini experience since that time in your life? What happened after the experience? Did anything change for you in your life, or were you further awakened in some way?

As for the practitioner not using the same points again, it has not stopped the ability of your Kundalini to be activated in the future. He obviously facilitated its rising during your session.

Q. Is Kundalini rising related to spontaneous combustion?

A. It's all the same force, you see. It just manifests itself in different ways. So yes, Kundalini is related to spontaneous combustion because it changes the chemical composition in the body. Remember, Kundalini is a flame of fire within us.

Source is saying that even in cases of spontaneous combustion, there is still a soul process going on that is very personal to the person experiencing it. Not every Kundalini experience creates spontaneous combustion, of course.

Kundalini can totally change your physical body; there are chemical and hormonal processes going on; there are nerve and brain changes happening and the organs and Chakras work differently—it is all quite dynamic on many levels. Whether Kundalini rises slowly or is a spontaneous full blown experience, it is still a process that can change your biology and consciousness.

Q. *Speaking of spontaneous combustion, what is it?*

A. I'm watching a process, so give me a moment. The word I keep hearing is 'implosion.' I'm hearing that it's a particular chemical reaction that happens inside of a person and it is very rare. I can't explain the chemical reaction, but I can tell you it looks like it happens very oddly, where chemicals collide with each other. An odd combination of chemicals that have gone awry. When that happens, it causes a spontaneous implosion inside the body. This is what I'm seeing—chemicals converging that create new reactions in the moment. It's not like it builds up for days.

Q. *When a person turns their body into light, can they ever incarnate or take on a physical body again?*

A. God actualized beings who can turn themselves into light at will, can come and go into materialization any time they choose. They would not need to come through the birth cycle to be born into a body. Instead, they can materialize a body of any age or appearance anytime and anywhere. This type of individual can also teleport, bi-locate or be in multiple dimensions at the same time. They are a fully awakened, deliberately decisive being.

In other words, they are their own authority in their full God Presence. Keep in mind this is God's intention for all of us.

God Men have achieved their freedom in the true sense, meaning that they are not subject to any laws or physics, but are in their unlimited God Presence.

Putting this in perspective, we have been shown that Kundalini is a God force within us that is our own Spirit energy, which has given us a very big piece of understanding about our innate Spirit selves. We see that our Spirit selves are not automatically *God-realized*. Each has a journey to go through to refinement, to maturity, to become an *adult* in the God sense. It is not unlike our children who contain our DNA, but who are unrealized in their birth state. They grow and develop through different stages physically, mentally, emotionally and spiritually. They make their own choices and have their own results. They can progress or digress as they choose. Our Spirit/Kundalini self within is much the same. It lies dormant in its immature or unrefined state and must travel the Path of Courage to become mature. Actualizing our God Flame is the ascending path.

Chapter Four

Consciousness

Consciousness

❦

Aingeal: "As I was saying the opening prayer, a beautiful bright white pillar of light illumined the room."

Q. *What is Source's definition of 'Consciousness'?*

A. "It is the ability to know yourself and know Me." In this answer is an ability that is *embedded* in us. The ability to have consciousness has been gifted from the Creator to every life form. This does not mean that every life form has the same degree of consciousness, but the ability to have consciousness is built into every living thing. Consciousness implies the ability to know ourselves and knowing ourselves implies *purpose*. The purpose of consciousness is to know yourself and to know Source. Consciousness is the ability to be alive and awake, to be aware of surroundings and to *perceive*—definition, form, structure and order. It is also the ability to perceive knowledge, to love and to extend Love.

Q. *Where and how did Consciousness originate?*

A. Source says consciousness originated from It, the original I AM. The I AM is Source's definition of Itself. consciousness originated in the I AM and is inherent in the I AM.

Q. *How do we think?*

A. We think from our I AM Presence and by God awareness. We organically have within us an awareness of God Source.

Q. *Are the mind and Consciousness one and the same?*

A. No. The mind (small m) is the alter-ego that came into being through varying degrees of awareness. Varying degrees of awareness make perceptions, which make a view of reality that is different for each person. Even though everything has inherent consciousness, not everything is awake to consciousness.

Source is distinguishing mind and consciousness from each other. Mind is something that is invented by *perceiving*, particularly by perceiving outside ourselves. By perceiving outside ourselves, we build a false self that Source is calling the alter-ego. This is the 'mind' that Source is talking about. Our view of reality is determined by each of us, by how and what we perceive and this is determined by our own unique level of awareness.

Q. *Is there a difference between the Ego and the alter-ego?*

A. The true EGO is the I AM Self that Source created; the original being coming from Source. It is the Truth that is inherent within each of us that we do not realize or remember. We need awareness to become self-realized. Because we are all at different levels of awareness, our perceptions of ourselves are limited. Therefore, we define ourselves based on our perceptions or level of awareness at the time. The alter-ego is the self that gets *made up* through limited awareness and perception.

Coming into God Realization is the remembering of our true EGO Self. Our True EGO Self is our I AM Presence. It is also called our 'True Organic Self' (see my first book, *A Time of Change* ~ *https://links.ahonu.com/atoc* for a detailed explanation of this term). In the process of remembering our True Self, we first have to undo the alter-ego self we have constructed through many lifetimes.

Q. *How does 'individual consciousness' compare with 'group consciousness'? Is there a relationship between them? How do we resolve this relationship?*

A. 'Individual consciousness' has to do with your own perceptions of reality. It is the collection of your own thoughts, beliefs and associations through your various experiences in life. It extends into your past lives and includes your collective soul impressions. Throughout your many and various lifetimes and sojourns into other dimensions and planets, you create your own imprints based on your experiences and your choices. This includes positive as well as negative imprints.

Anything we have not forgiven holds us back from higher awareness. When we address the issue of forgiveness, we really address everything that has happened in our soul stream. Where there has been a lack of forgiveness or love, there is still unresolved imprints. You can't go into Unity consciousness with judgments of any kind. Unity consciousness implies there is no separation between yourself and everything else.

'Group consciousness' is the collective set of beliefs of everyone in the group. In other words, it is an agreement of beliefs and concepts about reality within a group. These group agreements create a physics for a given dimensional space or planet. As long as the group agrees to these beliefs and concepts of reality, this will create the laws they operate under as well as the forms species become.

If the group mind were to collectively change its concepts or beliefs about reality or about what is possible within their given dimension, it would alter the physics or laws of that dimension.

The *relationship between personal and group consciousness* is that there is a common agreement beneath the surface about the reality they are in. They agree to the limitations and boundaries of their dimension. Still, it is possible for an individual to go beyond the beliefs of the group mind in their individual spiritual journey.

Q. *What is 'True Reality'?*

A. 'True Reality' is the I AM Self that is pure Love. Nothing else is actually real. Our limited perceptions and ideas about what we can be aware of at any given moment of time makes up pseudo realities, dimensions and planes of existence. It also makes up the planes of existence after death. Our limits in perception and awareness create false realities because all thought is creative at its own level. It's the alter-ego self that does this because it does not have full God Realization of its Self. When we finally arrive at our I AM Presence, we are back in 'True reality'. In 'True reality', you *are* all knowledge where perception is no more.

Q. *What is Actuality'?*

A. 'Actuality' is what we create through our experiences, ideas and perceptions. We all have the ability to be creative, therefore, 'actuality' is what we actualize, or manifest.

Q. *How do reality and actuality relate to Consciousness?*

A. They relate in the *process* of becoming self-aware. We are on a journey to greater and greater awareness of our I AM Presence. Reality and actuality relate to consciousness in the sense that they are helping us in this awakening process. Since we are talking about 'actuality' in the sense of what we *manifest*— playing with manifestation, coming to the place where we realize we manifest and create experiences—all this is part of the process on the way to becoming God Realized. There will be a time after we play with manifesting when we will naturally seek for things that are more 'real'. The satisfaction that we get from manifesting things externally will be temporary. This doesn't make it wrong because it is part of the waking up process. However, because the satisfaction is temporary, it will make us inquire more and more deeply into what is true and lasting. Therefore, 'reality' and 'actuality' are both stepping stones on the way to deeper and deeper Self-realization, which is true consciousness.

Note: *In this answer, the term 'reality' is the reality we make up with our perceptions; it is not the 'True Reality' spoken of earlier.*

Q. *What is the 'Subconscious'?*

A. The 'Subconscious' is what we decided and continue to decide is true but are not consciously aware of. Throughout our life experiences, we make conclusions and associations about life based on what we experience, how those experiences affect us and what we decide is true about 'reality'. These conclusions are stored in our subconscious as we continue moving through each day and have new experiences. We forget the conclusions we have come to about 'reality', yet they are still alive and active beneath the surface of our awareness. This is termed the 'subconscious'.

Q. *What is the 'Unconscious'?*

A. The 'Unconscious' is that which *denies that it is*. Deciding to be unconscious is deciding to be in denial of yourself, or 'what is'. The 'what is' can be on many levels. It can be a part of us that denies God within us or denies what's true in our lives, e.g. denying the truth of how you feel, denying what's really going on in your relationships, your career, or your health. It can be the part of us that doesn't want to know the truth.

Q. *What determines what we think about?*

A. Your individual perceptions and also divine inspiration. Our own perceptions formulate what we think about or what we focus on. However, there is also a mechanism inherent within us that allows us to receive thoughts directly from the Mind of God, which is considered 'Divine Inspiration'. This mechanism is called the 'Holy Spirit'. Thoughts and ideas come to us from higher places or levels of knowledge through the Holy Spirit of God within us. Both of these things determine what comes into our awareness or what we think about. We also have the ability to tune into the thoughts around us in our environment. These could be the thoughts of others or Nature. We can also be influenced by negative entities who send us negative thoughts.

Q. *How does thinking work?*

A. It works by awakening to consciousness. Thinking is the result of the ability to be aware of thoughts, which is consciousness dependent. Even though consciousness is embedded within us, it still needs to be awakened. Once this happens, thinking is a natural result. It is easy to see then, that not all life forms have the ability to think in the same way. In general, it can be said that consciousness, light and sound is what generates thinking.

Q. *Do animals think?*

A. Yes, most animals think but they are not aware enough to formulate thought. For example, humans have the ability to formulate thoughts and actively decide, whereas this process does not go that far with animals. Animals have the ability to think and receive thoughts, but they don't generate them actively and deliberately the way humans do. They have the ability to observe, feel and sense acutely and react accordingly. The ability to think and reason is dependent upon a particular life form's level of awareness. You can see this evidenced in humans even though not every human is at the same level of awareness or consciousness. The ability to reason, think and decide is not the same for everyone.

Q. *Do plants think?*

A. Some do and some don't, based on the same information we've been discussing in the prior question. What's missing here is the ability to *reason*, as with animals. Having said that, plants have the ability to be aware at the level of the group consciousness, or Nature. This is not an awareness of the I AM Presence, but rather an awareness of the field of Nature at this 3D level. Animals and plants do not receive divine inspiration. Their thinking processes are at the level of Nature.

Q. Does everything have Consciousness?

A. Source is saying "Yes", although some things have *history*, but not Consciousness. Some things are inert and have not gained self- awareness. Even though Source is saying that all things have *consciousness embedded within them*, not all things have the same potential for self-realization.

A rock, for example, would have come into being by things acting upon it from outside of itself. Some forms come into being by other elements being pulled to them or from their being pulled to other things. This process causes a level of form that Source is calling *inert*. These types of forms come into being as a collection of history or a collection of a series of events. These forms are too compact or dense to have consciousness activated from within their forms. *They have no self-ability to awaken.*

These types of forms usually have to implode, explode or get worn down and return to light before they would have the potential to begin a journey of consciousness awakening.

Forms that are a collection of history, such as rocks and crystals, will carry the data of their journey, but will not become God Realized at the level of density they are. In other words, they have not developed the consciousness to be aware enough to make decisions or manifest.

Q. What does it mean to 'Know Thyself'?

A. 'Know Thyself' is coming to the awareness of your I AM Self. This is logical, based on what we've been discussing thus far. When we look at the fact that there are many life forms that cannot take on a journey of Self-awareness, it makes our present state of consciousness so much more sacred. What's different in humans, for example, is that we have evolved in consciousness to have the ability to become Self-actualized. We have the ability to reason, to receive divine inspiration and higher knowledge and to transform ourselves through the ability to think, choose and decide.

We also get catalyzed by things outside of ourselves. For example, as we are having this conversation, our consciousness is being acted upon by something higher than ourselves at our present state of awareness. We are interacting with one another by these questions and Source Itself is answering us. This is stimulating more awakening within us and helping us to evolve and expand into more God Realization. This can also happen by reading a good book or watching a movie, going to a seminar or experiencing a tragedy or a miracle. Everything in the Universe is being catalyzed constantly by various forces. This affirms we are in relationship with everything and in this relationship, we progress or digress each other.

This is where the alter-ego comes in and has the potential to mess things up for us. We have made an alter-ego sense of self. We have created a sense of identity based on perceptions, dogmas, beliefs and associations with our experiences. We have fallen into a false persona that is different from the I AM Presence that is our natural True Self. There will be a point, however, where we will begin to awaken to this realization and understand that we have to undo our false perception of ourselves. This is where many people are on their path—they are disassembling their preconceived ideas about who they think they are and beginning to understand that they have to go within to discover their True Selves.

This realization is something you come upon of your own accord. No dogma or teaching can do this for you. It's not anything someone or something else can give you. When this happens, we are at a decision point as to whether we want to continue to live as our false selves or awaken to our True Selves. There is no judgment by Source about any decision we make. It is entirely up to us whether we progress and expand in our consciousness to God-realization or stay around and play with the alter-ego. Every aspect of life is valid but we will come to a point where we will want true happiness and this can only be achieved by what is permanent. Our I AM Self is the only permanent self.

Q. What is the 'I AM Presence'?

A. The 'I AM Presence' is God and is the Flame of Source individuating and having consciousness. When you know yourself as God incarnate, you know the I AM Presence. Incarnate doesn't mean having a physical body. That is only one tiny aspect of it. Incarnate means *as God*.

Q. How can we come closer to our I AM Self?

A. Our decisions bring us closer to God Realization or take us farther away. Our spirits naturally prompt us to awaken to more of ourselves. This prompting can be felt as a gnawing or questioning that occurs from within to know more about life and Truth. That is, we will have a need to discover or feel a restlessness that won't go away. We'll have the feeling that where we are isn't enough, or that we're missing something.

It can also manifest as a feeling of being stuck where we know we need to move forward or move on, but we're confused about what to do or where to go. Unfortunately, the alter-ego will have us go searching externally for more gratifications, while the real gratification can only come from knowing who we truly are.

You can see there are many aspects to this journey. We build a false sense of self, we play with experiences, we play with our manifesting abilities and we search for Truth. Ultimately, when we find that none of these things fulfill us, we begin a real search for our true nature, which requires that we undo our false personas and achieve virtues upon our path. We will be tested and tried to see if our resolve is sincere and if we have the willingness to continue. We have to become truly honest and examine our motivations for everything. We begin to realize how important our choices and decisions are in their effect upon our goal. We become disinterested in mind games and manipulations and focus our attention on being more sincere, real and loving.

When we finally begin to realize and actualize our True Self, we will only be interested in *being* Love and extending Love.

Until we get to this place, we will continue to play in false realities. We will continue to reincarnate and have lifetimes in other dimensions and on other planets. I mention this because I want us to realize how big this journey is and how much of the alter-ego is in existence and to what extent it continues. We only end up 'Home' back in our True Selves when we naturally arrive at the place where it is *all* we desire. This has to be a natural process—it cannot be forced—otherwise it is not authentic. It needs to be said again that there is no judgment in this journey with all its ups and downs, false personas, learning and experiences. It is all part of the process of becoming and awakening to more consciousness.

Some people have no interest in finding out that they have made a false persona. They are not at a consciousness level that would naturally push them to seek higher. They may be at the level of consciousness where they only desire to experience mundane or material things. If this is what their consciousness can hold, this is where they will be and there is no judgment in it —it is perfect for them at this stage. The desire to *know* will be something that occurs from within, as a restlessness or questioning of one's existing reality. The search will have begun at this point. This is when one will desire to meditate, go within, or read and learn about esoteric knowledge.

This search will also allow you to see the relationship between your outer and inner worlds. You will begin to see your outer world as a mirror reflection of your consciousness. You will begin to see your beliefs and opinions playing themselves out in your everyday experiences through your relationships and situations. You could ask a question of a higher part of yourself and see the answer being played out in your 3D world. Before this, you may not have seen this relationship or noticed answers coming to you from a variety of sources. You may not have been paying attention in this way, but now you see it. It was there all along. This is evidence that you are coming closer and closer to remembering your I AM Presence.

* * *

Q. *Do our Guides and Teachers use our dream state to communicate with us?*

A. Yes, they do. Let me tell you a story. A few years back I lost my sister. She came down with a strange illness and within six months she was gone. We had a phone conversation a few weeks before she died when she was feeling better. She told me that she had two dreams of my brother Chris, who had died when he was 22, many years earlier. I thought this was very strange, as none of us had dreamt about him all this time. I had a fearful feeling when she told me this, that this somehow meant he was coming for her from the other side. She too thought it was very curious that she was dreaming of him. She told me that while in the dream she said to him, "Why haven't you come to me before now?" He said, "Because you've always been so busy."

This answer makes the point that when we are in our 3D lives, we are so busy thinking and working and focusing our attention on other things that we're not aware of things going on in the spirit state or on other levels. Our Guides and Teachers sometimes can't get their messages through to us because our attention is focused elsewhere, so they use the dream state to attempt to get their messages through.

If you keep a dream journal and record your dreams upon awakening, you will realize that everyone and everything in the dream is some aspect of yourself. You can find out a lot about what you're being shown in this way. This process can improve your life and make you much more aware. It is a wonderful way to get to know yourself on other levels, since dreams will often bring forward activities that are going on in the subconscious mind. They can also be messages from your Higher aspects.

In my sister's case, it can be seen that spirits coming from the other side can also be bringing messages. In her case, seeing my brother was letting her know that she was preparing to leave this world. I didn't want to believe it at the time, but she passed three weeks later.

In most cases, dreams are a symbolic language that we can interpret when we begin to ask what is being symbolically represented by the sequence of events in a dream or by who is appearing in our dreams. Since we all make associations with people and events in the sense that we give them all the meaning they hold for us, we can inquire into our own symbolic associations with the 'players' in our dreams and recognize it as our own internal language to ourselves. If you take the time to do this process, dreams that may seem to mean one thing when you awake oftentimes turn out to mean something very different upon reflection. This can be especially true if you have a bad dream and wake up fearful. However, if you take the time to go back and look at the series of events in the dream and ask yourself what those events and actors mean to you, oftentimes you will see that you're being given a very positive message—possibly one of transformation or of a situation needing resolution or a decision needing to be made. In these cases, the fearful dream can be a wonderful tool to change your life in a positive way.

There are many levels of dreams and many things that can be going on in the dream state. I won't go into all of them now, because Chapter Four deals entirely with dreams.

Q. *Does gravity have any effect on our consciousness?*

A. What I am hearing is that gravity is the *result of* our consciousness. Gravity changes according to the consciousness of the masses. In other words, our collective beliefs and levels of consciousness dictate how much gravity is in a particular place or reality system. Gravity doesn't affect our consciousness; our consciousness affects gravity.

Here's an example: When people have images of ascending, it is always that we are ascending out of gravity or out of time-space. We become so light that we move beyond the effects of gravity and the limitations it seems to impose. In actuality, we become free of it.

We each have the ability to go beyond the gravitational field of time and space by shifting our own consciousness to a higher, more loving state of being. Our consciousness keeps gravity in place for us until we change it.

When your consciousness becomes in alignment with more and more Truth, it will hold more and more light within it. The more light we can hold, the less gravity plays upon our bodies. This means, if the mass consciousness of the planet continues to awaken further, gravity will also shift in its properties. Have you ever noticed that people who are highly evolved in their consciousness don't seem to age as rapidly, or they seem to float along as they walk? This shows that the effect of gravity on their bodies has lessened.

If the collective consciousness of a planet or Solar System has a very limited perceptual range about its reality, its process of manifestation will be very slow.

We have witnessed recently however, that when an individuals consciousness shifts, their ability to bring manifestations into the material plane speeds up. This is a good example of how the shift in consciousness is affecting the gravitational field. When the gravitational field is dense and slow, it takes longer to see the effects of our consciousness materialize.

Q. *How can we build wealth with our consciousness?*

A. Source is saying that there are several levels to this answer. First of all, it is the alter-ego self we have created that wants material wealth. We can manifest wealth by our thoughts, by our imagination and powers of visualization. We'll need to look at the limiting beliefs we have that may be interfering with the attraction of wealth and then reprogram our belief structures into positive wealth *expectations*. Our powers of visualization are incredible. We underestimate the power of our imagination and imagery to bring things to us. Wealth can be very easy and we have a tendency to make it too important.

Putting it in perspective, the material wealth that most people desire is a desire of the false self.

Having said that, there is still nothing wrong with it and no judgment around it. Having it or not having it can be part of our awakening journey.

There are so many stigmas and fears around having wealth that we have to look into ourselves and make the necessary changes so that our subconscious gets a positive message about having it. Asking yourself what you want wealth *for* will determine what happens to you in relation to it. When you use your imagination to manifest wealth, you also must manifest keeping yourself in balance with it, otherwise you will lose it. Another point is to acknowledge money as having consciousness and asking yourself these questions:

1. Do I have a conscious relationship with money?
2. What is the quality of my relationship with money?
3. Do I express gratitude, respect and appreciation for money?
4. Do I consider money a friend or an enemy?
5. Do I accept money is just one reflection of my consciousness?
6. Do I know all supply from Source flows *through* me?
7. Do I recognize that the Universe and myself are one?
8. How well am I able to accept that I am made in God's image?

Balance is very important in any process of manifesting. We need to know what our motivation and purpose is for our desires in order to hold the balance of having what we desire and the responsibility connected to it. Anything we can imagine can come into manifestation. The truth is that Source doesn't care if you have wealth or you don't have it. If you want it, Source says, "Have it!" We are speaking of the material level of wealth. The higher form of wealth has to do with our ability to love everything. Being in love with everything is also the ability to be in communication with everything and see the interrelationship of all life.

It is an act of feeling deeply without censoring. We become part of the abundance all around us by being in harmony with it and by accepting everything as ourselves. We become sensitive to life on very intimate levels and our intentions are completely harmless. This results in feeling complete love and peace with everyone and everything. In this state, prosperity happens naturally and flows through all levels.

It is important to be honest with ourselves and acknowledge what level of wealth consciousness we are at. If we're in the consciousness of the alter-ego which believes if it acquires more wealth, it becomes bigger and more important in the world, we can manifest that false persona for ourselves. If we desire wealth for security purposes, that's alright too. Let's not deceive ourselves into thinking that material wealth is our ultimate key to happiness. We understand money can make life easier on material levels. Just be aware however, that the world of the alter-ego is a temporary world that holds no permanent happiness or peace of mind. There are responsibilities that go with every state of being.

If you are moving toward the true EGO and are headed toward understanding your I AM Self, you will arrive at a different type of wealth in which abundance on all levels flows naturally and easily. It is called 'Love'. This path has purification of the alter-ego as its directive.

Q. *Do we interact with others we know when dreaming?*

A. Certain parts of the brain shut down and other parts turn on while we're sleeping or dreaming, so it is very possible to interact with others while in these states. You can communicate with people who have crossed over or with people who are here in 3D, if you are mutually agreeing to an experiment to see if you can meet in another dimension in the dreamtime. You can also meet other aspects of yourself in other dimensions while you're in the dream state.

* * *

Q. *Should we meditate and how do we do it?*

A. Meditation, according to Source, is really the decision to 'Know Yourself'. There are many types of meditation and people have different purposes for meditating, making the result dependent upon what your motivations are. For instance, Ahonu learned Transcendental Meditation™ many years ago. He was looking for inner peace after the death of his first-born son. His meditation was focused on going to a place of peace and solitude within. When I meditated, I would call on my Higher Self and ask to be taught. I was looking for knowledge and truth. I would lie on my bed at the same time every day while my children were taking naps and call on my Higher Self to teach me. Then I would wait. For the first two weeks I didn't receive much, only some flashes of color. Eventually those colors turned to symbols, which turned to telepathy, which turned to journeys into other dimensions. My meditations became a mystical path in which I was taught about developing virtues and overcoming my alter-ego.

In one of my journeys, I went to a dimension where I saw a higher aspect of myself teaching a classroom filled with students. I realized that each one of those students was another aspect of myself. There were males and females of differing ages and many nationalities represented. The progress I made was due to my practice of making time every day to be taught.

Meditation is a decision to set time aside to go within and discover your inner world, whether that is a more peaceful centered state or a rich landscape of knowledge of other dimensions. If you are practicing meditation daily or twice a week, you will eventually come to the place where there is no separation between your inner and outer worlds. All life becomes a meditation. Meditation is not complicated, but it is a practice of putting yourself in a quiet receptive state. Many feel meditation is difficult because they cannot stop the thoughts that come in, so allow the thoughts to come in. They will eventually leave and then there will be no more thoughts coming in.

Ahonu: I have done over 20 years of meditating of several different types. Two of these types are 'concentration' and 'contemplation'. The 'contemplation' type is where someone is contemplating Scripture, for example, or contemplating the Sacred Heart of Jesus or other various types of sacred literature or objects. 'Concentration' is another method, where you concentrate on your breathing or on a candle flame or some other object.

Transcendental Meditation is different from these two types in that it doesn't concentrate or contemplate. It attempts to make the mind blank by focusing on a mantra in the short term until the mind arrives at a state of nothingness. There are differences in all these ways and, as Aingeal Rose said, there is no right or wrong way. Just be clear about your purpose for meditating because that determines the result.

Q. *What actions will build a life of fulfillment and joy in 3D?*

A. Source is saying that you will not be able to have a life of joy and fulfillment until you can love yourself fully. When you don't love yourself or you make choices that are self-destructive, there will always be guilt and fear attached. There are small things we all do every day that we know are not in our highest good. These could be on any level of life.

Loving yourself is a huge piece of the puzzle on the way to becoming harmless in your intent toward all life. Harmlessness is what gives us a life of fulfillment, because we become in love with everything and that is what joy is. You look out and see beauty and love everywhere. You don't get upset over the many little things that occur during the day that perhaps aren't perfect. You know that all is well and your intention toward all life is innocent and benevolent. You have no more desire to harm or judge anyone or anything, especially yourself. Your internal guidance is in harmony with your 3D life at this stage and you know what to 'do' clearly and easily. Therefore, the action to take for this is the willingness to look at the alter-ego, because it is inevitable it is going to die.

The pretend self, the self we make up, the self that we measure will disappear. The alter-ego tells us that we will be happy and fulfilled when such and such happens, if this person does this for me or if I attain measurable success; if I have that perfect relationship, wealth or security. Joy and fulfillment to the alter-ego are all dependent upon outer experiences, successes or accumulations.

Of course, you can enjoy life and have all of those things, but remember the journey of consciousness. Challenging yourself in the outer world to demonstrate accomplishments can be an important part of you becoming self-aware. The balance comes when you understand that the outer world is not *you*—it is merely a reflective stage where you get to act out your desires. There will always be a point when the inner gnawing or restlessness to 'Know Yourself' will return.

This restlessness is inherent inside of you because Spirit desires to take you into the knowledge of your true EGO. It wants to return you Home to real and lasting love.

On the journey of life, you will find that material things do not bring you a sense of fulfillment and joy or lasting happiness. You will begin to desire things that are more permanent, such as inner peace, love, giving and a deep connection to all life. You come to the place where you realize that the outer world is a dream where thoughts and beliefs play themselves out. It has no permanence of its own and it fluctuates, depending upon beliefs and feelings. This realization can relieve a lot of unhappiness if it helps you to stop searching for happiness outside yourself. This does not deny that things happen in the dream, but it will put it into perspective as we see that we are making up our perceptions as we go along. They rise and fall and rise and fall, over and over again, proving that there is no lasting permanence to them This is why the foundation of the alter-ego self doesn't last. It fluctuates and changes on a whim. If a person bases their identity on the alter- ego, they will be very vulnerable indeed to anything that destroys their idea of who they think they are or disrupts their 3D reality.

There is no lasting happiness in the alter-ego with all of its accomplishments and losses. The only thing we are really looking for is the Love that is everlasting. I'm not talking about love as in relationships, but Love as the only True Reality of which we are made.

Q. *What is the 'Higher Self'?*

A. The 'Higher Self' is the same as the Holy Spirit inside your mind. It bridges the gap between your alter-ego and your True Self. The Higher Self, or the Holy Spirit, is the *memory* of Source within you. There is a point in your conscious evolution where you will actually *become* your Higher Self. When this occurs, the need for the bridge disappears and you will be in direct communication with Source Itself.

Q. *Would God's consciousness exist without my consciousness?*

A. Source is amused by this question. Yes, Source's consciousness would exist without our consciousness. Source IS consciousness. It was there before we were created.

Q. *What gives us the ability to communicate with trees?*

A. The trees are saying that it's because they desire to communicate with *us*! This implies that communication is a two-way street. We all have the ability to communicate with everything. We could know the entire history of the Universe by picking up a stone and communicating with it. The ability to communicate with everything is built into us. However, not everything *wants* to have a conversation with us, but there are plenty of things that do.

The ability to communicate with trees happens because the trees desire to converse with us. Conversations imply giver and receiver and without one or the other, the conversation would not happen.

Let's distinguish between 'communion with all life' and 'conversations' with other life forms. Communion with all life is the recognition and experience of being 'All That Is', while *conversations* with other life forms is a separatist perception where there is a giver and receiver exchanging thoughts or feelings.

Q. *What is a practical way to become self-aware and conscious?*

A. Source is saying that the first thing to do is to have the desire to 'Know Yourself'. This may not sound like a practical application, but we have to remember what comes to us in our perceptual field is a result of our desires and thoughts.

For myself, I learned much through my meditations, but I also kept a daily journal and I inquired deeply and honestly into my own associations and beliefs. I was very interested in how my thoughts created my experiences and how they played out in my relationships for positive or negative. I was willing to explore deeply into myself. I needed to confirm that my associations produced a manifestation in the outer world.

As I journaled, I found many thoughts and associations that were causes of the conditions in my life and I had memories of past lives surface that were affecting my perceptions in the present. Once I saw this, it gave me the opportunity to redefine and change my subconscious programming. When I saw the reflection of the change appear in my outer world, I began to realize that *everything is consciousness*. This led me to create an online course on *Transformational Writing*, so others could learn this method if they desired.

So, begin to inquire about everything in your life. If you wake up in a bad mood, sit down for five minutes with a pen and paper and describe your mood. Ask yourself what this mood represents or means to you. Every emotion and mood has an inner association. We give things all the meaning they have for us. If we find we've made a negative association with something, we can change the *definition* into something positive that serves us.

This is all done by journaling. It is one of the most powerful things you can do and one of the least expensive. It will transform your life by leaps and bounds in just minutes. Self-honesty is crucial to this process. We all have a dark side that is not nice and can be very judgmental. Being honest about this in our learning process helps us move out of judgment and realize that we're no better than anyone else. Seeing this and being honest about this leads to compassion and understanding for ourselves and others. This is a necessary process in clearing the way to the Love that has always been within us.

If you truly desire to shift your consciousness, the first and most important step is to have the desire and willingness to inquire or meditate. You can also partake in energy work that is designed to help shift your energy and awaken your Higher Centers.

Chapter Five

1) Time & Dimensions
2) The Future

Time & Dimensions

Aingeal: "As I'm saying the opening prayer, there are many spheres at the ceiling level. These are not orbs, but moist and liquid *spheres*. Some look like they're shimmering with silver, some with gold and some with white. They feel aware and I feel a consciousness with them. They are from a different dimensional space, not familiar to me. I've not encountered them before."

Q. *Is there a specific number of spheres in the room?*

A. Yes. There are five or six that are popping in and out of our dimensional space; they look like a Christmas ball with an elliptical shape in the middle. They're being really clear about their shape, but yet they feel moist.

Q. *Are these spheres other aspects of ourselves?*

A. No, they are not other aspects of ourselves. Even though I'm feeling them here, they're not coming down *into* our dimensional field. They're outside of it even though I'm aware of them. They do not want to come into our time net for some reason—they're hovering right at the edge.

Q. *Could they get trapped here?*

A. Yes, and they don't want to. They have a particular moisture that makes me feel that they are not compatible with our environment.

* * *

Q. *What is 'Time'?*

A. 'Time' is being shown to me as a living web of light and sound particles that is a vast consciousness field.

It becomes dark beyond or outside of it. 'Time' *curves*—it's round and it arcs. It belongs to a certain dimensional space in that it has boundaries, which is what differentiates it from the darkness that I see beyond it. It is made up of a living web of consciousness and energy; all of our thoughts and desires are there. You can go beyond it into a void or hyperspace, although hyperspace doesn't have anything to do with the time matrix that I'm looking at.

Q. *How many other dimensions are there inside and out of planet Earth at the present time?*

A. There's an unlimited number of other dimensions intersecting our reality. We don't have any concept of how many dimensions there are in, around and through us.

These dimensions intersect our third-dimensional reality, appearing as vertical and diagonal lines that intersect our dimension at different angles. Some of them go right through our dimension, crossing over it or just passing through it. They don't affect our dimension and we don't notice them because their frequency and angular rotation is very different from ours. Some of those dimensional spaces don't originate in our time field. We could be aware of them or fall into them however, at the point where they intersect our time web.

There are stories of people who have visited places where some past historical event occurred and they reported seeing a scene from that event playing itself out in living color, as if it were just happening. The scene would appear with the same figures from the past, dressed in their period clothing and re-enacting the same event as if it were still alive and locked into a time warp. Those visiting the place felt as if they were in a strange portal watching an alternate reality take place.

Some people experienced it as being out of their bodies, where they popped into and back from a different dimensional space. The only way you can experience another dimension in your 3D waking state is if you're at that point of intersection where our 3D and the other dimension meet. If you weren't at the point of intersection between dimensions, you wouldn't be aware of anything unusual.

Q. *Is that dimension just an altered state of consciousness?*

A. The effect of being in a portal could produce an altered state of consciousness, but the altered state doesn't produce the portal.

You can also experience your alternate selves in other dimensions. You could come upon an intersection point where another you is in another dimension, and you could experience that as a 'living now' timeline.

Q. *Can we get out of time?*

A. Yes, time is definitely something you can get in and out of. It actually has an edge or an arc to it.

Q. *Does time stop?*

A. Time is a living consciousness made up of our consciousness. It's not going to stop until we stop—until we ascend out of our perceptions of this physical reality. We may see it change its properties, however, as mass consciousness changes.

Q. *Does the boundary of time expand, contract or stay constant?*

A. It seems to stay within fixed dimensional limits or within certain parameters. I don't feel that it expands. It has a certain frequency range, or belt. It is round, it has an arc shape, like a disc. It feels held in place by other forces in the Cosmos.

If you look at the Earth spinning on its axis, around the center is a big, elliptical energy field. If you were to tip the Earth the other way, you might get another elliptical the other way. Time feels similar to that.

Q. *Does time have a heartbeat?*

A. It is more of a breathing rhythm as opposed to a heartbeat, similar to an in-and-out breath.

Q. *Can time speed up or slow down?*

A. I'm getting a '*no*'. It's not going anywhere, but stays within its boundaries. What people perceive as a speedup or a slowdown is really just a *ripple* in time. Think of it as a big energy blanket with a woven pattern of light that can ripple and vibrate at different rates. It's a fluctuating field. When you encounter a ripple, it can make you feel as if things are speeding up or slowing down. You could experience time as speeding up today, but tomorrow you might think it has slowed down. It's not a stable field in this sense, but it is stable within its parameters.

Q. *Are we multidimensional and could our mental body be in one dimensional space while our emotional body is in another?*

A. I have to be very careful here with words. I can't say that it's that separated. Source doesn't want us to think of ourselves in that way. What I'm seeing instead is a pillar. I'm looking at cells in the pillar—the different aspects of us are different cells in the pillar. The pillar is complete and all is contained within it.

Source doesn't want us perceiving that parts of ourselves are separate realities, because they aren't. It would be easy to think that way because different parts of us may function at different rates of vibration, but all our bodies are contained within us. It's not the same as having an experience of an alternate self in a different reality.

Your emotional and mental bodies are contained within your own pillar of light. There are a wide variety of experiences in the time field and what we perceive dictates what we see. We may want to call them 'realities' but Source wants us to call them 'experiences'. There are not different realities in the time field, but there are definitely many different perceptions and experiences there and many other sets of realities *beyond* the time field. How you think and perceive determines what you tap into.

We don't see beyond the time field because we are locked into our beliefs and perceptions about time. Our frame of reference for reality has limitations at this point. It's only when people release their attachment to the idea that the time field is fixed that they actually start to have an experience of what it's like outside of it. The time field is what holds your body together. Beyond it, you wouldn't have a body at all.

Q. *Are time and matter synonymous?*

A. Matter comes together *because* of the time field, which holds matter together. This is exciting because when people ask, "How do you dissolve your body into light?" or "How do you walk through a wall?", you do that by dissolving the time field *within your consciousness,* and it won't happen unless you understand that. Most of us are locked into a frame of reference about time, which is why we can't seem to shift matter. The stories you may have heard of beings materializing or dematerializing are factual because they have freed themselves from the time field. They can reassemble their material form by coming back into the time field. They get in and out of time.

Q. *Is an alien abduction actually a dimensional shift or an altered state of mind?*

A. An alien abduction is an experience in another dimensional space out of our time field. It is not made up in a person's mind.

Q. *Is it the same as an altered state of consciousness?*

A. This is the same as the above question. No, it is an actual experience. The alien abduction experience is occurring in a dimensional space that intersects our time-space but is not *in* our time- space. The abductors can manipulate the properties of our time-space in order to get in and out of it. In an alien abduction experience, the person is taken temporarily into another dimension and then returned. The person is having an experience in the alien's reality and then brought back into this one.

Some abductees have experienced seeing a blue light. When the door opens, that blue light shines into our reality and people experience it wherever they are in this reality. Not every experience of blue light relates to alien abductions however, because the properties of blue light are also involved with the art of teleportation as well as many other spiritual experiences.

Q. *So, they're opening up a dimensional portal?*

A. Yes, and they slip through that interface.

Q. *Was 2012 an interface, or an exit point to another dimension?*

A. No, 2012 was not an exit point and did not push us out of time since then. It was more like taking the blanket of time and shaking it, giving all of those little filaments that are woven in the web a chance to rearrange themselves. Because they rearrange themselves, things can look, feel and function very differently.

Time as we know it will start to have more of these shifts. Since we're in the blanket of time, we're going to ripple with it and experience reality in different ways. What we see will be different because the old pattern is being shaken up. It has actually been shaking for some time and will continue to shake. Individuals will have different experiences, depending on their own state of consciousness.

We're still not out of the time field, but the carpet of time to which we cling is being shaken.

Q. *Can we get out of time during this process?*

A. As I consider being 'out of time', I feel like I'm in hyperspace. Being beyond time is bigger than you can imagine. You may experience a very expanded state of awareness, but you're really not out of time until you can dissolve your body, materialize, dematerialize and teleport yourself. Our consciousness can catch a glimpse but we won't *actually* experience being out of time as long as we believe we are locked in our bodies. We can only have a limited perception of it.

Q. *How do we enter hyperspace?*

A. Transcend your body beliefs and perceptions as explained above. Time looks like a giant dimensional wheel. When you start to get into hyperspace—and I'm getting very hot—you become one with 'All That Is'. Your perception of yourself as a being with a particular identity disappears. In fact, perception itself disappears and only pure consciousness remains. So, when you ask how to get out of time, the answer is that you have to get off the *wheel* of time, which is all about the perception of identity that creates karma. It's about perceiving yourself as something different, separate and distinct from something or someone else. In perception, you are in relationship with something or someone, as opposed to *being* All That Is. I have to be clear—it isn't that you dissolve into the Oneness and have no awareness. You literally *become* everything. You no longer define yourself as any *one* thing, because you're everything.

Q. *Is that zero-point?*

A. No, zero-point is an actual location.

Q. *Is zero-point beyond the time field?*

A. Yes. When you say 'zero point', I have an experience of traveling fast in hyperspace heading toward a center, which feels out beyond this time field. I'm having the sensation of going into a funnel; I'm going in and in and in, and I'm not coming to the end yet. I'm going inward and I'm going to be arriving at a point. I'm heading in toward something that is either a starburst or a sunburst. It's a point of interchange or interface. Zero-point would be that concentrated point of energy—if you can call it energy—or a point of intensity that is an interface to an entire other reality field or world.

Q. *Is this what is called a black hole?*

A. No, I'm not in a black hole. The point that I'm heading in towards is not black at all—it's bright!

Q. *Is it Home?*

A. Going Home is going into the field of 'All That Is' and would not be going to zero-point; it would be *becoming* 'All That Is'. That's Home.

Q. *Is that where zero-point ends?*

A. No, because there are many zero-points in the Universe. In terms of the one that belongs to us, I'm heading towards this bright point, and then I'm at this burst, which opens up into an entire other field of life that we don't know about, because it isn't in our time frame. It's not in our experience of time. So, as much as that would have an intersecting point, there might be another zero-point somewhere else where the same process happens. Zero-point is being explained as a concentration of energy that's an interface point. The Universe is so huge that even in our broadest perceptions, we can't imagine.

Q. *Is Tír na nOg real? (Irish myth, the Land of Eternal Youth)*

A. I'm seeing it as being in a different layer, or overtone above our Earth. It has an elliptical shape—the same shape as the time field—and it rotates the same way, but it's at a different resonance, which is why things there stay in suspension.

You can go there, but I honestly don't think that you'd want to stay there forever—it's not a desirable place to stay indefinitely. It's a place where you could get caught. If you were there—you'd want to change and continue to grow and expand. Someone could desire to go there and could create that for themselves, but once they got there, they wouldn't like the unchanging nature of the field. They'd be cycling around in it eternally.

Q. *What happens in déjà vu?*

A. When we sleep there is a part of our consciousness that disengages from our body, but is still connected to it by a myriad of threads. Our consciousness floats off and has experiences in other states. *Déjà vu* is when the physical you here in the third dimension catches up to the experiences your consciousness had while you were out of your body.

Q. *Can we experience other dimensional spaces?*

A. Yes, we can experience other dimensional spaces by making the intention while in a meditative state. The focus to experience other dimensional spaces sets the grids in place that allow you to get there. Ask yourself, 'Where do I want to go? What do I want to experience?' There are some dimensions and many random holes in the dimensional field that you definitely would not want to experience, so, be careful what you ask for. Another option is to ask for a dream to show you a dimension that would expand your experience of Source. *Quantum Jumping* is another great way to experience your other selves in other dimensions.

* * *

Q. *Are there dimensions from where you might never get back?*

A. It could happen. If you found yourself in a not-so-nice dimension, the experience could be so traumatic that you may not realize that you're the one who put yourself there and that you can also choose to get out of it. You may get caught in the fear of being in it. When you're traveling in other dimensions, you need to have your wits about you concerning coming back. You need to be able to declare, 'I'm going back now.' You could easily lose control of that faculty if you suddenly found yourself immersed in a hellish place.

Let's talk about fears for a moment. I knew someone who made the intention to experience a specific aspect of himself in another dimension. His intention was positive. However, when he opened the door to the other dimension, he was met by a negative spirit. He closed the door and assumed his travel to the other dimension wasn't working. Nonetheless, he tried again and was again met with a negative scenario. I talked to him about any fears he might have had about going to another dimension. Sure enough, he had various fears about it. Once these were dealt with and cleared, he was able to successfully meet other aspects of himself in other dimensions.

Q. *So, if I were to end up in one of those hellish dimensions, would that correspond with some aspect of my own consciousness?*

A. Yes, as in the example above. It is important to have your intention be clear and to be sure that you are not being wishy-washy or fearful. Otherwise, it would be better to wait until you may be more ready.

Q. *When we talk about people with wisdom and spiritual knowledge, does that equate to different levels or dimensions?*

A. It equates to achieving a higher frequency level of awareness. You could have a person with much wisdom and spiritual knowledge and they could still be living here in our 3rd dimension. Integration of knowledge and experiences occurs within you, which is similar to something being *woven*. The degree of integration one acquires brings you to a place of balance and understanding within yourself, which is called wisdom. You now have knowledge, which is what wisdom is based on. This is not book knowledge, but knowledge that comes from integrating experiences. A person who is wise has integrated knowledge within him/herself.

There are beings in other dimensions who could have experienced or learned more and integrated more. Integration of knowledge catapults you to another level of *awareness*, thus changing your frequency level.

Q. *Current physics is concerned about the amount of dark energy and dark matter—what are they? Science postulates that 96% of the Universe is missing. Could other dimensions explain it?*

A. 'Dark energy' and 'dark matter' are two different things. Dark energy is appearing like tubes or cylinders of other dimensions or realities. They look hollow and are vertical. They co-exist in our time web and are interwoven into it. They're part of our time web, but because they're cylindrical or tube-like, they're not accessible in the same way that an intersecting or angular dimension would be. Other dimensions and realities intersect at angles and you could most likely find the angles and the exact points of intersection. Dark energy however, looks like cylindrical, vertical tubes that intersect our time field and then go through it. Because it's cylindrical, there's no intersection point. It's difficult, but it looks like an alternate reality that has a shape that isn't based on angles but on a cylinder or a tube.

Dark energy hasn't been defined, because it doesn't fit into the web of time neatly in terms of degrees and angles. It doesn't have the same dynamics or shape that we're used to. It is a cylinder or tube without any door. It might spin around inside itself and it might move, but you can't access it.

Dark matter has to do with a vacuum. Dark matter are particles that are vibrating at a heavier rate than light would be. Light particles sparkle and dance. Dark matter feels heavier and has a magnetic quality to it. I get a sensation of being pulled into a vacuum by it. It's a different type of particle. It's still part of what makes up everything, but it has different properties and wavelengths, even though it is still part of the 'stuff' of Creation. Everything's different in it—the spin rate, the electricity and the magnetics. I feel it in the bottom of my feet—it's a buzzing feeling. What's its function? The qualities of it are responsible for making vortices. In other words, the spin rate of dark matter makes vortices. It can coalesce things into form. It has a motion to it. Gravity would be connected to dark matter because it has a force that can pull things into form. I keep seeing vortices with a vacuum-like effect. Scientists know more about dark matter than they're telling. They're already using it. It's actually connected to gravity and anti-gravity.

Q. *Is technology a dimension where we could get stuck?*

A. It depends on how it's being used. Technology is learning about different properties and how to use them. In other words, whether technology advances in a certain way depends on how scientists put together the properties they discover. It could either be something that traps people or something that allows them access to other dimensions. Technology itself is not another dimension, but it can be a tool to access other dimensions.

Q. *So we're not at risk of getting caught up too much in computers and mobile phones?*

* * *

A. It depends on what we're using them for and what kind of frequencies they emit. All low frequencies weaken your immune system. The dependence upon artificial things also dulls your innate communication with your higher aspects.

Q. *Is there more information from the moist spheres?*

A. They've turned creamy-white and they're shimmering.

Q. *What are their names?*

A. They're *places*, not persons or beings. They are reality fields. They have a consciousness. They can hover above our heads and not be caught in our time field. They can give us an experience of another realm of consciousness. They're alternate realities from higher, expanded states.

We can try an experiment if you like. Put your hands above your head. Ask them to come over your head and see if you can feel them. They feel like they have skin and they're watery—like a water balloon. They're saying that they're an *opportunity*, because they come from a reality that is not affected by our time matrix. Because they're not affected by it, you'll be able to access healing waters and keys which are in the form of little sound shapes that come directly in and give you the experience you are asking for.

So, if you're asking for knowledge, a healing or clarity, they can download that to you. *To be clear, they themselves are not coming into you.* They're really clear that there's nothing about them that's will come into you because they're outside of our time matrix. It is an opportunity for us to experience a different type of information and access an experience that you wouldn't be able to access in our current reality field.

Q. *Can everyone accept this opportunity?*

A. Each person decides if they want this experience or not. I already accepted. I can feel it, so I know it's positive.

If you want it, accept it. It's not like anything I've ever seen or experienced. The shape feels cool in temperature. They're watery, but this water's different—clean and regenerative, like an elixir.

Q. Can we access it now?

A. It's above your head now. The more you use it, the more results you'll have because they are conscious, aware and alive. It's a collective, so it wouldn't want to be called one thing. I don't feel that they come to everyone and their appearance is not a common thing. I feel a skin, like a bag. I feel hot from experiencing them and yet they don't feel hot.

Q. Can we give this gift to others?

A. They're telling me, "No, it's for you." However, by being in communication with them, you can make intentions for others.

Q. Have we been given this opportunity because we chose to come here with an open mind and ask these questions?

A. No, it's because of the topic, *Time and Dimensions*. If we weren't having this topic, they wouldn't have come in. You could say they are another type of consciousness, but they're not locked into our time field, which is why they can intersect it and cause different things here without becoming involved in it. I think there's great learning from them as well. All you have to do is focus your intention and you could have a question and answer session with them. You each can have your own personal relationship with them right now.

Q. So, the more we keep asking these kinds of questions, the more we open up to knowledge?

A. Yes, questions promote knowledge. If you don't ask the questions, how would you know? It's the topic. They came because we're discussing *Time and Dimensions*.

Q. *Is there anything they want to tell us that we haven't asked?*

A. Each one of us has to focus in to get our own answers. We'll do it right now. Ask the question: "Is there anything they want to say to you or to the group?" Let's all focus on that.

Time is taken for participants to have their own experience...

Aingeal: They're readjusting everything in my body. Quite interesting. They're saying it's like having your higher brain. I could feel the water in my body adjusting; my heartbeat is being regulated. I'm totally peaceful and relaxed now. They showed me places in my body where I have held trauma and they are fixing it. They kept saying, "Higher brain. Higher brain." I feel as if it were a higher brain that we all used to have. The higher brain looks like it is filled with pulsing light—glowing with beautiful, yellow light; it is much bigger than the brains we have now.

Participants:

"A song just stuck in my head, 'Burning down the house.' It burned down all of my assumptions, expectations and perceptions. I am all of that: I am time and I am no-time, I am zero-point, I am beyond the dimensions, the whole lot. Anything I want to think of, anywhere I want to put my consciousness or focus or intend."

"Restraining your imagination is like applying a vice onto your life." That's the first thing I got. The next thing was: "You bought in. Now buy out."

* * *

"You accepted an extraordinary thing tonight. Now continue to accept extraordinary things."

"Recognition is gratitude. Gratitude is recognition for this consciousness." I got a final piece of advice that said, "Meditate more."

"It was like looking down at all this."

"I feel that the whole experience of time is a collection of people's ideas and beliefs and an experience of watching ourselves create."

"I feel like creation goes on forever. It is so big that we just can't fathom it. Even when you get out of this particular time field, this is only one small field. You're never going to be tired. You'll love being part of everything. It's just so, so amazing. What's the point of it? I feel joy and fun."

Q. *What is the point of Creation?*

A. From Source's point of view, Creation is joy. Source says: "Isn't it wonderful, isn't it awesome?"

We have no idea, because we've made ourselves so limited in our perceptions in this time field. If our perceptions were freed, we'd see everything as joyful and magnificent. Even within our own field of time there's so much to see. However, compared to what I'm seeing, our time field is a very sticky field. We have a lot yet to know.

The Future

This chapter explores the concept of the 'Future' and how it works. It is not about what's going to happen in the Future, but the *idea* of the Future itself.

Aingeal: "As I said the opening prayer, I saw a rosy purple color with a line of royal blue with a white line around it. The rosy purple color usually indicates things having to do with karma, hardship or suffering—things we have experienced in our lives. It's an interesting color for this topic."

Q. *What is Source's definition of 'Future'?*

A. 'Future' is an *idea* in the Mind of God. This means if God did not intend for life to continue, there would be no possibility of Future. *All* Futures are based on ideas that coalesce, unravel, coalesce and unravel again, continuing forever. We are looking at cause-and-effect. Ideas create the continuation of Future as we perceive it in our dimension. It looks similar to a dreamscape. I'm in clouds of color, which seem to be people's ideas, thoughts or concepts that float and become cloud-like. They get generated from mind and they travel together in a horizontal frame of reference where these clouds move forward. On one hand I'm getting a fleeting feeling with it, but on the other hand, I'm getting pictures of physical events manifesting. So, the Future, being an idea in the Mind of God suggests an implied Future is inherent in the desire for Creation. In other words, Future is a continuation based on Source's desire for life to be.

Q. *What makes the Future? I understand it is built on ideas or perceptions, but what makes it concrete?*

A. What makes the Future happen, or coalesce into an event or manifestation, is simply thought and desire. As long as we have thoughts and desires, we will have a continuation of a Future. Every thought and desire creates a form of itself on some level. In other words, thought and desire make things continue and become concrete.

Thoughts and desires manifest as pictures or imprints and the more energy they have, the more they become concrete. We are going back to the fact that we are creators and because we are creators, we have within us creative ability and creative energy. Our thoughts and desires continue this imaging, or creative process. The power of our creative imagery coalesces with the elements that are around us and makes things come into form. Every thought and every desire takes a form or shape on some level.

Now, some thought forms dissipate if they're not very powerful. They may be ideas that can coalesce into a little cloud and then dissolve, whereas other ideas which are heavily energized, make stronger manifestations. This is because our thoughts and desires create a magnetic field and begin to cause the elements or substance in the Mind Field to coalesce around them, creating a plasma field in which the thought or image begins to take on form.

Source says we create a Future because this is how we think.

We are thinking from past to present to future and many of our thoughts concern the making of a future. They are about what we are going to do tomorrow, in the next hour, in the next five or ten years of our lives, or what's likely to happen on our planet. Our thoughts are creating the Future because we *focus* on it. If we were not focused on the future, we would most likely be in a true *Present Moment*—we wouldn't be creating future scenarios. It would be quite a different experience.

You may be wondering what happens when you're in a True Moment. Source says that if our thoughts were not future or past oriented, we would be eternally in a *Presence*, which would give us a very different quality of experience because we would be in direct communication with all life *in the moment*. It would be a blissful existence from moment to moment. Source is saying that this is really where your true power is. Power is in being *in your Presence*, in each moment; you're not directing your thoughts toward creating a particular future or a particular plan. Instead, you are immersed in the lifeforce energy of the Moment, which is the direct connection to God and bliss.

Q. *Is our Future predetermined if we do not deliberately focus our intent on creating it?*

A. Let me qualify 'predetermined'. Source says the future is predetermined *to an extent*, because God intends that life 'be and continue'. However, the kinds of futures we create ourselves are predominately continuations of the past—past beliefs, predictions, prophecies, programming, *etc.*

The future is predetermined to a point because we've been thinking so long about it and there have been many things predicted about the future. Therefore, people are *expecting* a future, so a future continues. In a way, it is predetermined only because there are so many thoughts in the ethers that have been future directed and are still in a process of coalescing and have yet to become manifest. So, there is a hodgepodge of futures based on people's thoughts in the past—centuries ago, as well as today—that have long been coalescing into futures.

So, when I asked Source if It has predetermined the future for us, It says that Its predetermination has never been about events, but always about bliss. In other words, It has predetermined that the experience of life and Creation has been for us to experience complete bliss in every moment.

Source looks at 'Future' as if it's synonymous with the word 'eternal'. 'Eternal' is being present in each moment in complete bliss.

Source is also telling us that being in the Moment is itself an eternal experience and the experience is not static because the Mind of God is full of joy, happiness and expression. We don't know what that is because our minds are busy thinking about the past and worrying about the future. We are rarely in a Present Moment and because we aren't, we don't get to experience what God's Eternity is like in each blissful, joyful Moment.

God does not have future 'events' planned for us. That is something *we* do with our own consciousness by thinking linearly. What Source does do is hold the Eternal Future of bliss for us whenever we redirect our consciousness to the Present Moment rather than to the past or the future. If a person is not consciously directing their future, it will unfold according to their beliefs, thoughts and programming. It will also evolve astrologically, according to their birth chart if no conscious changes are made. In this sense, their future is predetermined.

Q. *Are the past, present and future all the same thing?*

A. Only in the sense that they are all based on thoughts that we're thinking. Say you're using your present moment to think about your past. What you're doing is bringing that event into all of your present moments and your future moments. In this regard, past, present and future are the same thing. It all depends upon where your consciousness is focused or on what we continually think about. It isn't that the past *is* the present or the future, it's that we recreate it to be one continuous event. You could say that your past is in your present and that your future is assured because of what you're thinking.

In other words, you will re-create past events to appear in the present, which then appears again in the Future. It is a function of where your perception is oriented and what you energize with your thoughts and desires.

Here is another example: Let's say something traumatic or blissful happened to you when you were a child. If your consciousness is built around those events and has a strong memory of them, it will keep repeating the same patterns or the same type of experience. In that way your past, present and future are all the same because you're focused on a particular type of event or experience. Your experience might express itself a little differently, but the underlying pattern will still be the same.

Q. *Can we travel into the future and if so, does that mean it has already happened?*

A. That's a good question. Well, it has already happened on a particular level because of what we're talking about today. In other words, because we've already focused on the future, an event has already been created from our thoughts and we may not *encounter* the experience until its expression or manifestation happens in 3D. If you continually think about the future, all those thoughts and desires go out into the Mind Field and become expressed in some form at some time, depending on the kind of energy they carry. So, if you travel into your future—which you can do in meditation—and you look at yourself in the future, you can see the effects of your thoughts. You can see how your thoughts are coalescing into the future. In this way, some parts of your future have already happened, but they may not have manifested in this particular density yet. When you go traveling into the future, you're at a different dimensional frequency than you are when you're in 3D.

It is the same thing that happens in a *déjà vu* experience—a part of us wanders off into the future and has experiences while we're sleeping . When we wake up, we forget where we've been but when our 3D reality finally catches up to that journey, all of a sudden we re-experience it—we realize that we have already done this, or been to a future, which we have.

Q. *How can we change the future?*

A. That's another good question in relation to the answers we're getting tonight. There are levels to this: If you travel to the future in a meditation and you see a particular scenario unfolding as a future, you can redirect the forces or the elements to manifest a different outcome. You have to tell it to rearrange itself into a different outcome. This is interesting because we're looking at the part of us that is truly a magician. If you move into the future and you're watching something unfold that you don't particularly like, you can say, "This is not the outcome that I desire." You can define whatever alternate outcome you desire and you can redirect the elements to manifest by your conscious intent alone. So, yes, you can change the future, *but only if you're consciously in the dimension where it's manifesting.*

When you see the results of past thoughts manifesting in your everyday life, you can redirect that manifestation as well, but it has to be done consciously in the Present Moment, as it is happening.

Q. *Has everything already happened?*

A. Source is saying "No, not everything has already happened, because people are still thinking—thoughts are still being thought and desires are still being generated."

I'm a bit surprised by this answer because many people believe everything that could happen has already happened, but I'm not getting that. Source is saying "No, because consciousness is unlimited and the ability to imagine is both unlimited and ongoing." It may look as if there is nothing new under the Sun, but that is the result of perceptions that haven't truly changed for centuries. However, if we had the ability to truly be in Presence, in the present Moment, we would be in an eternal and unlimited experience of blissful expressions. Unlimited because God is still thinking! God's Mind still has thoughts.

Q. *Does the future only happen because of time?*

A. Source is saying, "No", because time is only the result of our thinking. It is there because we are perceiving past, present and future. If we were *not* thinking past, present and future, there would be no time. Time is a concept that we create by thinking linearly, i.e., horizontally. It's very different than being in the Present, which is a vertical or moment-by-moment orientation. If you were truly there, you would not have thoughts of past or future, therefore time would not exist for you.

Q. *What is a 'Moment'?*

A. Source is giving me an image of a droplet of water. I'm having an experience of it. It's hard to describe, because I feel a great amount of energy rushing toward me and surrounding me when I ask this question. This feeling is indescribable and hard to express in a one or two word answer.

However, Source is defining such a 'Moment' as pure pleasure, which seems to be the *effect* of the Moment, while the Moment itself is an energetic experience. If I start to put an explanation to it, I am not in it anymore, but I will do my best.

It's like being totally and completely aware of yourself. This tremendous energy is coming toward me from all sides, surrounding me and it feels as if it keeps moving inward toward a 'center' in me. It is concentrated and focused into a center point where there is a huge awareness not only of self, but also of everything else at the same time. So, the Present Moment has a motion to it, because I feel as if I'm moving *in*. Instead of an outer focus, I am going inside, which brings me feelings of complete pleasure and bliss. You have to experience it yourself, which you can do just by concentrating on, "What is a Moment?" which is the question I asked of Source. There's huge power in this—huge energy and peace. It is as if you're more alive than you've ever been with an awareness of your existence that is completely internal, but yet you are aware of everything.

Because of what I am feeling, I can understand what Source is saying about Presence being bliss. I can see how our focus from past to present to future is an entire 'other' reality system that we've created with our minds based on a linear view that precludes an experience of a True Moment. It is like a camouflage on reality that we've created with our minds. I am realizing that the energy coming towards me from every direction is my *own* energy and personal power *returning* to me, as I take my focus off the past-present-future.

Q. *Will there always be a future? Will humanity always think in this horizontal way?*

A. Source is saying that the futures we create may last for a very long time. People like to use their minds in that way. Until we have more people shifting their focus to the Present Moment, we will see futures created from the past. As we can see, hardly anyone is in the Present Moment that Source describes, so you will see our version of futures continue until all people shift their minds to the Moment.

If you use your mind to conceptualize a false reality and you are thinking about the past, present and future, you are creating scenarios that manifest as those futures. You can create beautiful experiences or you can create horrible experiences. It's all about the quality of your fears, beliefs, perceptions, consciousness, and all of the mass collective as well. This also relates to world events. What we all collectively use our consciousness for manifests as world events.

Source is still smiling, because It knows it is all one big dream. What we're doing with our consciousness, in terms of the linear way that we do things, is a dream. We create illusions, ideas and images which manifest as events that we call reality. The illusion is that it isn't the Reality that Source is describing when we're in the Moment. Source's Moment is a True Reality—a blissful, eternal, pleasurable intention from the Mind of God. There is incredible power in it, which we would be experiencing if we were in the Moment. In other words, we would be experiencing true Creation as Source intended it.

We don't experience true Creation because we have too many concepts built on false ideas about reality and what we think is important. We teach our children whatever we believe, so patterns continue. It could end if everyone suddenly decided to turn inward to the Moment. It could end our dreamscape futures. Think about all the people who are having and raising children with their own beliefs, telling them what reality is, how the world works, how they have to believe and behave in this religion or that and how a good education is required so they can make money. Such ideas have been handed down for generations.

The ancients worshipped the Sun as God, then they worshipped Nature as God, then they believed that all the Anunnaki gods were the real God; then there was Yahweh, Jehovah and Allah and on and on it goes. Every time parents teach their children a religious or scientific belief, a military perspective of conquering or protecting a boundary, they are teaching them to co-create the future the same way they did, so the past repeats itself.

Q. *What about the future of the Earth?*

A. Source is smiling at this question too and It's saying, "Now isn't that an interesting game you've made for yourselves? You can destroy this Earth or turn it into a Paradise."

This is where everything that we've been talking about comes into play. This question might put the *idea* of time into a different perspective for everybody. Again, our thoughts coalesce into physical events in our world because of centuries of past thoughts which *makes* time. Densification of a thought or manifestation starts with the thought itself. We see cartoons of someone thinking and a little cloud appears above their head.

Think of thoughts and desires as those little clouds. Each little cloud of thought get's energized over and over. If the mass consciousness keeps focusing its attention on particular thoughts or scenarios, the cloud gets bigger and stronger and at some point starts to materialize and coalesce in our 3D reality. Eventually, it is an 'event'. There is usually what we consider a time lag between what people think and the event that manifests as a result. Something could become a future event in our time frame because of collective thoughts from a century ago.

This is why we're interjecting the idea of becoming conscious. When you become conscious, you understand that you can *de-energize* old thoughts so that their potential manifestation collapses. You collapse time so you can create a new future through your conscious awareness.

The waking up process allows us to be keenly aware of our thoughts and change them in the moment. We realize that our thinking will manifest a future in its likeness, which is why there's so much emphasis on examining our beliefs and judgments, what we fear, what we think about, what we worry about, *etc*. We donate those thoughts to the collective consciousness as well as to our own personal futures. Of course, our positive, beautiful thoughts get donated too!

It takes a lot of people changing their minds to collapse a mass future event, but again, I'm hearing that if one person was truly conscious of their power as a creator, they could collapse events by changing their thoughts around it. God smiles at our perceptions about the future of the Earth because it is determined by what *we've* been thinking about, which is why it's unfortunate so many people are focusing on the end of the world —storms, plagues, destruction, bad weather and Armageddon.

We are witnessing such disasters now, but how long have people been predicting this? You can go back into the 1800's, 1700's and before, and you can find many ancient predictions about what we are experiencing now. When did those fearful thoughts start in people's minds? For how many centuries have people been believing the same sorts of stories?

People to this day still energize these scenarios from their religious traditions and books. Then it cycles around, the consciousness changes its mind and declares that we don't want the world to end! You can see how people in the past have helped manifest what we are experiencing now, but we can still undo negative prophecies in our present.

If we are conscious and we stand up and are aware, we can say "No, no, this is *not* going to be the way it is!" We can use our power to say, "We are creators and this image is *not* the unfolding of events that we would like to see on Earth. We choose this vision instead…"

If we create a new picture that the Earth is a blissful, beautiful place, we are consciously, deliberately interrupting the old paradigm of war and suffering. We can all do this. You can do this in your own life as well, but remember that all this is still within the context of the dream. Creating a positive Earth future is still within the context of dreaming *linearly*, whereas, if we were truly in the Moment, we would be experiencing something totally different—we'd be in the blissful moment, which would automatically be creating more bliss as the continuing result of our being in the True Moment.

A lesson in *A Course in Miracles* says, "My salvation comes from me." In this lesson, Source declares that the healed mind does not plan, which is what we are talking about today.

We plan because we're afraid of the future. We don't truly believe that being in the Moment would sustain us by the Love of God Itself. In my experience today of being in the Moment, I was astonished by the power and peace that rushed toward me, which is a very different experience from what we're doing linearly.

Q. *Will there be more disease, storms or wars in the future?*

A. The way our consciousness is moving, people don't want any more big wars. I think we're going to see more avoidance of war. As for diseases, it looks to me as if the mass consciousness still has much self-educating to do because it still believes in things like vaccines and pharmaceuticals. We will keep creating diseases because we have not cleared our consciousness about it, which is really an imbalance within the self. Our consciousness regarding disease has not changed much, so diseases will persist. The masses are still turning their power over to pharmaceutical propaganda. Consciousness is changing slowly, but as I see the momentum of this change, I still see much ignorance about disease.

We take disease too seriously. For example, when a person comes back from the doctor with a diagnosis of cancer, the collective energy around cancer is that it equals death. Most think that someone with cancer will soon die, when the truth is that cancer is toxicity—an imbalance in the system. There are emotional components to it as well, but it can be unraveled with selfcare, detoxification and nutritional diligence. There are many alternative therapies and many people survive cancer.

Regarding storms, we are watching the Armageddon scenario play itself out in the collective mind, but we don't have to. Source has been saying that we don't have to experience more Earth changes—we could immediately see a pristine Earth. We are all creating climate change because of old beliefs that go back thousands of years. We've all heard that the Earth goes through Cycles—a Dark Age, then a Golden Age.

We are watching this purification process happen as the darkness works its way through. What would it be like if we all stopped believing in Cycles? What would happen if we all used our consciousness to be in True Moments instead?

There is a correlation between the way we think, what we believe and what happens historically. Our repeat consciousness is why history repeats itself.

Let's take Nature as an example. We believe that animals killing one another in the wild is natural and that consuming food is natural. We believe we have to keep killing and consuming, that this is the natural way, the way animals are and the way Nature keeps the balance. Nobody really knows what a mass consciousness living in a True Moment would produce for animals and people. Certainly the animal that is being brought down by another and killed is not in a state of bliss—it feels pure fear and is not in God's bliss. So, we have a lot to think about with this and about how we use our consciousness.

Our consciousness creates the future, so as long as we think the above is normal and this is the way it is—tides rise and tides fall, people live and die and we accept this as normal—we will keep creating futures like this.

Going back to the topic about Source and Original Creation, Source was implying that we have no idea of the true love power of Creation. We don't know what Source's Creations of love are. There's an expansive experience that is very different.

Q. *Can we visit the future through meditation or dreams?*

A. Yes, you can travel into the future in dreams. One way is to use CDs that teach you about Lucid Dreaming. This process helps you be awake in the dream state and mold the outcome of the dream while you are in it. Another way is meditation with the intention of taking a look at *your* future. A psychic reading can give you a heads-up on what kind of future you are manifesting for yourself. Quantum Jumping is another useful tool for exploring the future.

Q. *Can we affect the outcome of a major illness by having more positive thoughts in the present?*

A. Yes, of course. However, there are many reasons why people get ill. Some of it is negative thinking, toxicity, trauma or inherited illnesses. There can also be soul lessons going on with some illnesses, in which case positive thinking may not have any effect.

Q. *In the future, will we have more activated DNA strands and can we affect that now?*

A. The more you take time to be in the moment, the more all of that happens in the moment. So, again I am going to talk to you from two completely different reality perceptions. To answer your question in the *linear* perception where we keep our consciousness focused on past, present and future—we think of our DNA as an evolving process that we can activate as we change our consciousness and our emotions. Science has proven that emotion changes DNA, so clearing up issues that are binding, limiting or confining will activate other parts of you. Once you free yourself from limiting perceptions, you will create cells and chemicals that reflect your state of mind. The body responds to your ideas, beliefs and what you think is possible. We also have help on the linear side in the sense that there are things going on in the Cosmos that are stimulating DNA evolution, which is evidenced in the Indigo, Crystal, Rainbow and Golden children. With their extraordinary gifts and intelligence, these children have more DNA strands active.

The next reality is going into the Moment, which most of us have not truly experienced and which may seem unreachable, but only because we haven't focused our attention there. If you focus on the Moment and have an experience of it, it will erase the Evolution idea and replace it with a timelessness that is eternally creative and in likeness to the Divine Will of Source.

PART 3

Chapter Six

Angels, Archangels & Ascended Masters

Angels, Archangels & Ascended Masters

Aingeal: "As I was saying the opening prayer, the room filled with many small flames of fire. They belong to each one of us and they're suspended in the air above our heads. They may have something to do with our topic today."

Q. *What are 'Angels'?*

A. They're emanations or expressions of the Rays of Source.

Q. *Do Angels fight?*

A. They are smiling at this question saying, "We don't fight, we have discussions!" They don't fight in terms of what we would imagine as emotions of anger and the like, but they have lively conversations. I feel no anger from them.

Q. *Are there Angels on Earth?*

A. Yes, billions! They aren't exclusive to Earth, however. There are some here in physical bodies and some that are not and they can be in many other dimensions at once. We all have a Guardian Angel. However, our Guardian Angels do not take on a physical form unless it is for a particular temporary purpose.

Q. *Is the Angel Gabriel male or female?*

A. Predominately female, but all Angels carry both essences.

Q. What are 'Archangels'?

A. Archangels are masterful Angels who have been appointed by Source for specific functions. Angels and Archangels differ in that Angels are rays of light that are very soft, loving and gentle in their nature and are an extension of God's Rays. They have various personalities or aspects which can be quite varied. Archangels are beings that are masterful in certain arts and they have divine appointments or missions to uphold God's Plan for Creation in some way. You could say they are adept in the arts of the Creator. They are appearing very tall and huge and more defined in density than what I am seeing as Angels, which are more of an emanation of light.

Q. What are 'Ascended Masters'?

A. Ascended Masters are beings who have evolved in their spirit/soul consciousness and have achieved varying levels of mastery. They have had many lifetimes in many dimensions and planets, including Earth. They have developed skills in manifesting, healing, transmutation, de-materialization, physical immortality, higher sciences and the arts, to name a few. They have achieved Individuated mastery in these ways, but would still be evolving in their spirit selves.

Q. Is there a Hierarchy of Angels?

A. They don't use the word 'Hierarchy'. Rather, they have different *purposes*. There's no hierarchy in terms that one is better or higher than another. However, there is a difference in their Individuated vibration, mastery and purpose. Some have achieved more knowledge and expertise than others, but they do not consider themselves superior to other Angels in any way.

Q. *Do Angels intercede for us?*

A. Yes, Guardian Angels can and do intercede for us as often as they can. They always show up when babies are born. There is an Angel appointed to each individual to help them fulfill their soul purpose. We recognize this Angel as the Guardian Angel who will accompany them through their lifetime.

Q. *Do Angels have different relationships with humans or can one Angel be all things for one person? Do we have a wealth angel, a health Angel or a protector Angel?*

A. When we ask, "Are there specific Angels for specific purposes?" I'm hearing from our Guardian Angel that It would like us to have a better relationship with *It*. This one Angel has been assigned specifically to help us fulfill our soul purpose. This covers all aspects of our soul journey—protection from things that take us off our path, guidance in career, *etc*.

Some Guardian Angels appear as warrior types, some as loving and gentle and others as wise guardians. The type of Guardian Angel chosen relates to the individual's soul purpose.

Our Angel can't do everything *for* us—however, it can and does help with the things we need to fulfill our soul contract. The fulfillment of our contract is affected by the decisions we make along the way. Our Guardian Angel will carry the tools, qualities and attributes needed to help us fulfill our contract. Of course, their guidance can be thwarted by the free-will choices we make.

Q. *Are there Angels of Karma?*

A. Yes, there are Angels of Karma, but let me explain. They are Angels you encounter after you die who help you with your life review. You can call them 'Angels of Karma' in this sense because they help evaluate the life you've lived when you leave this Earth. I do not see Angels that are judges or that keep a record of your transgressions.

Q. Do Angels take on form?

A. Angels can and do take on physical form in certain cases for specific reasons. In these cases, the purpose for taking on a physical form determines how long they stay in form. It could be for a moment, hours, days, months or a lifetime. Angels are mainly spirit beings. They sometimes make themselves known to people as rays of varying colors, depending on their specific qualities or attributes.

Q. Is there a difference between Guides, Mentors and Angels?

A. Yes. True 'Guides' are most often people who have lived other lives on Earth or other planets and are now in spirit form. They have gained various degrees of knowledge and experience and have been given the assignment or opportunity to be Guides for people on Earth or on other spiritual planes.

Many relatives can become Guides once they cross over and have grown in their soul experience enough to be allowed to be Guides, if that is their wish. There are times when a Guide can be in physical form and act as a teacher for a particular period of time.

There can be lower Astral spirits pretending to be Guides for people when they aren't, so discernment is necessary. These spirits can fool those who have limited skills of discernment or who haven't cleared their distorted beliefs and judgments.

False guides tell people what to do; they pretend to be saints, Jesus or other famous people. They will use people who are naïve, need their ego bolstered or are insecure. True Guides will never tell you what to do, but they will always lead you to the greater truths of self-mastery, love and healing. They help you face yourself and strengthen your ability to discern and choose. They may leave you for a period of time if you are meant to become more mature or masterful of your own accord. These times may feel as if you have been abandoned, but they are still very much aware of you.

Mentors don't incarnate on Earth, as they are higher-dimensional beings. They are a being from a person's Galactic Soul Family who is appointed to be a Mentor. They are similar to a wise parent watching you grow, experience and learn or help you fulfill a planetary mission. They influence you telepathically with thoughts and information. Their purpose is to watch and support your personal mastery and mission, while stepping back and allowing you to make your own choices. They, as well as your Guardian Angel, are present at your life review when you cross over. They also help you decide what your next incarnation will be when the time comes for you to come into another lifetime. They are masterful and appear as powerful beings who may also encourage you to go on missions not related to Earth.

Angels are extensions of the Rays of Source, as mentioned previously. They may be appointed to be Guardian Angels for the sole purpose of helping a person fulfill their soul contract. They would protect as much as they are able, deter negative influences, keep you away from as many regressive paths as possible and thwart relationships or situations that would hinder or set you back on your soul's journey. I say they do this as much as they *are able*, because they have to allow for your free will choices. If you have to go through certain experiences to achieve mastery, they will not interfere. Rather, they will protect you as much as possible throughout those experiences.

Other Angels who are not Guardian Angels, have other duties and purposes throughout the many dimensions between here and Source. There are Angels of healing, Angels of teaching and learning, Angels of music and the arts, Angels of science and geometries and on it goes!

Q. *Are there dark or fallen Angels?*

A. Yes, there are Angels who have descended and gotten caught in lower densities. If an Angel keeps descending to lower densities, Source no longer calls them Angels, but calls them 'demons'.

Angels that have fallen too far from Source no longer retain their angelic frequency. When I tune into fallen angels, I feel hot from the inside out and I see that demons are in a process of disintegration. By the time a being falls to the level of a demon, even though they wreak havoc, they are disintegrating from the inside. Because of this, they are limited in their effect and have a limited lifespan. Source wants everyone to be aware of this. When demons put on their big show to make people fearful, remember where they are on the scale of power!

Source is saying a demon's biggest ability is manipulation and lies. 'Deceit' seems to be the word for them. Their game is to deceive through people's mental and emotional bodies by putting untrue ideas or feelings in people to cause division. Remember they have a limited lifespan and need to take power from others to continue to exist.

Q. *Are there other ways demons influence us?*

A. They influence us through chaos and division. They like to cause and produce insanity and separation in people and situations. If a demon can give us negative thoughts or feelings and make us angry or make us crazy, they can then feed off of these emotional energies in us. We then contribute to creating chaos in our lives and in our world, which causes accidents, sickness, death and violence.

Still, we have to be really clear: *Demons don't carry much power of their own.* This is not to say demons are weak—some do accumulate tremendous soul energy stolen from individuals. Still, their influence is limited. because they have to use *our* energy to create havoc. They use our emotional and mental bodies to cause problems by instilling fear or confusion within us.

Here's an example: Let's say someone has just come out of a broken relationship and they're feeling heartbroken. A demon will use that opportunity to put ideas in the person's head to make them suspicious, angry, jealous or despondent.

In these states, the person will not be in control of their emotions. In actuality, we're sending out negative chaos balls. Anyone else who is vulnerable to the same thing is now influenced or affected by these balls. This is how war, divisions, murder, suicide and other catastrophes are caused. It is done through the implantation of negativity in vulnerable people.

I also see demons gathering around soldiers in battlefields. I see hordes of them over soldiers who are fighting wars. This is a major way in which chaotic forces are kept in place. So much of what they do is based on deception. They will hover over one soldier and then hover over another to create a mass energy of chaos through the collective group of soldiers. Demons themselves are not an army en masse—they use *groups of humans* to achieve negative power and force.

Q. *Do religions use Angels and Archangels in rituals?*

A. Yes, the invoking of Angels and Archangels has been and still is commonly used in rituals by religions as well as those who are performing white or black magic ceremonies.

Earlier we said that Archangels have specific assignments given them by Source because of the specific qualities and powers each one has. Those that do rituals know the qualities and powers of these beings and how to invoke them for their own desired result. *It is not the Angel or Archangel itself that comes to the ritual, rather it is the manifestation of the qualities and powers that occurs through the medium of words, elements and geometric arrangements.* The ritual itself will generate its own power. The Angel or Archangel itself does not come down to accommodate rituals.

What a person is really tapping into is the Angel's particular *frequency and qualities* for aid in manifesting a desire.

Q. *What is the proportion of good Angels vs. demons?*

A. There are more good Angels than demons. Let me explain it to you vibrationally. There are billions of good Angels and you could equally have billions of demons. However, their power does not compare. Angels have more power than demons. A billion demons is weaker vibrationally than a billion good Angels, making a difference in what each is capable of doing.

Q. *Are Angel Cards helpful?*

A. Anything that helps someone shift into a positive place is helpful. If the association a person is making with the information on the card helps them move positively forward in their lives, then it's helpful. Once again, it is good to remember that the Angels or Archangels that are printed on cards do not specifically come to people. It is the *qualities and attributes* assigned to the Angel that brings upliftment and shifts. It's not that they *wouldn't* come to someone, but not in the majority of cases. Most likely it is your own Guardian Angel who helps you choose the cards that help you the most.

Q. *If a person claims to be channeling an Angel or Archangel, are they channelling a demon instead?*

A. There are demons that could take advantage of that opportunity, but I wouldn't say all the messages people receive from Angels or Archangels are from demons. Sometimes a person could be tuning into their *own* angelic nature, their higher aspects or their own Guardian Angel. This is when discernment becomes very important. A higher being is always kind and loving and their presence promotes peace and compassion. They never ask for obedience or devotion, nor do they promote guilt or punishment in any way.

Q. *Do Angel pins protect the person wearing them?*

A. Yes, they can help protect because of the *intention* behind them. It is the intention that offers the protection, not the pin itself. The pin is a physical symbol of the intention.

Q. Do we see Angels when we die?

A. Your Guardian Angel will definitely be there! It has never left and never will leave your side until its assignment is over. Sometimes groups of Angels come to attend someone who has crossed, but not always. It can be the case for those who are Angels themselves returning Home to their Angelic family, or for someone who needs to go to a specific healing plane. All people will meet their own Guardian Angel.

Q. Do we keep the same Guardian Angel lifetime to lifetime?

A. Not necessarily. It depends on your soul contract. Earlier we mentioned that Angels have their own personalities and qualities—different 'wavelengths' is really what it is. You may have the same Angel or not, depending on what your soul desires to accomplish in a particular life. Remember, the Angel assigned to you at birth is chosen because it carries the frequencies or qualities that will help you fulfill your soul contract. This could change with each life. It is good to know that your Guardian Angel also progresses through the victories *you* make in your life and by its own efforts in its assignment with you.

Q. How does my Guardian Angel assist me?

A. Your Guardian Angel acts as a liaison between you and Source. It's interested in helping you establish a direct relationship with Source so you're able to receive clear information in any situation. It guides you by sending you thoughts that you receive as inspiration or new ideas. Your Angel prevents and deters harm. It soothes and comforts and reminds you that you are loved and important. You can begin a journal with your Angel and write it letters or pour out your thoughts and feelings to it. Ask it for what you need and pay attention to the little or big signs showing up in your life that let you know it has heard you. This works!

Q. *Can negativity override the power of my Guardian Angel?*

A. Negative influences can come in when and where you are vulnerable or weak. They use what you haven't healed in yourself to influence you. It reminds me of the old cartoons where the good Angel is on one shoulder and the devil is on the other shoulder. Both are trying to influence the person; the choice of which voice the person will listen to is up to them. If they choose to listen to the negative voice, they will fall into negativity. If they choose to listen to their Guardian Angel's voice, they will have help in overcoming their vulnerabilities. Everyone has their own power of decision. Indeed, we are choosing continually which voice we listen to. The power of our decision is very important.

There are many of us who pick the weaker position and believe, "I'm a victim in this situation. I'm down and out. I can't get out of this." There's a point of intersection between the two voices and it is *you* that has to make a choice.

When do negative forces get in? When we give up. Even then, we can still make another choice. Even if the negative gets in and we feel immobilized, we can still make a choice. That choice can simply be to ask, "Source, please help me!"

This is also the perfect time to ask our own Guardian Angel to intervene for us and protect us. We can also call on our own I AM Presence and surrender the situation to It.

I've been in situations when I have felt so horribly in despair that I felt paralyzed with no willpower left. I couldn't make a thought to save myself. In those dark moments, the only thing I could say was, "God, help me. Please help me." I would always be answered. Sometimes it was like a ray of light in my feelings or a new and brighter thought. Sometimes all anxiety left and I'd feel immediate peace. Other times, I'd be reminded of my power to create my own reality, so I'd leave my victim perception behind.

Still, other times someone would call or stop by, or offer me some healing assistance. Help can take many forms, so pay attention. It took me asking and making the sincere choice to be helped and to surrender.

I always surrender to God when I feel I'm in a situation that I can't get out of myself. I have no problem admitting I can't figure something out. It really is all about our decisions. Even if we say, "I don't think I'm consciously choosing the negative...", ask your Angel to show you the many times you could have made a different choice and you wanted to wallow a little bit longer in the negative. You will be shown how much you participate in staying in negativity. We receive much protection from our Guardian Angel—we are not aware of just how much we have been protected!

As to the influence of negative forces, we also need to watch the food we eat. We absorb the vibration of whatever it is that we're consuming. Our Angel will help us become sensitive to the vibrations of foods if we ask for assistance. We'll use meat as a good example. We know that animals are killed for our consumption. I've been around cattle and have seen them interact with their families. They know when something is wrong with a family member and they go through a trauma just as we would. It wouldn't be any different than us knowing that we're all in a line to be killed. Animals *know*. Think of the trauma and fear that is in an animal when it is being killed.

The other thing to be aware of and sensitive to is how foods are grown, treated and harvested. We spoke about this in great length in *A Time of Change* (*https://links.ahonu.com/atoc*). Shifting into eating foods that won't leave negative imprints in your energy field is a good practice. If you are a person who needs animal protein, try to buy meat that is humanely treated and killed as well as grass fed with no hormones or other chemicals in their diet. Remember to always bless your food with gratitude, whether you're a vegetarian or a meat eater. Try to choose only 'happy foods'—this is an intuitive exercise. Without any preconceived ideas about food, go into a food store and ask to be led to the 'happy foods' for you or your family and see what you gravitate towards. *Don't analyze what food you're drawn to—just allow.* It could be different each time you shop. This exercise requires you to trust your instincts.

Q. *How can my Archangel assist me?*

A. You don't have your own personal Archangel! What you *do* have is a part of yourself that is an Archangel Self in a higher dimension; it's a part of your own higher aspects on your way to God Realization. You don't have an Archangel assigned to you other than this.

Your own Archangel Self can assist you in that it can provide you qualities and virtues such as strength, courage, the ability to reason truly as well as the ability to discern greater truths.

I'm seeing steps to a ladder of ascent between the 'us' here and the part of us that's more ascended up the ladder. It's just an image they're giving me. If we put ourself on a rung of the ladder and climb up, we can put ourself in our own Archangel energy and feel it. It does not come down to us; *we* go up to it. We can do this through meditation as well. Eventually, the 'we' that is physically here will incorporate the frequency of our Archangel Self into our life as long as we are doing the inner transformation required.

Q. *What is the purpose of Cherub Angels?*

A. Cherubs Angels are very close to the elemental kingdoms and Nature. They work more with Nature than with people. They could be considered part of the elemental kingdom or the 'in-between' worlds. They can perform specific functions for us, however, when necessary.

Q. *What are Elementals?*

A. Elementals are the spirits of Nature—fairies, sprites, tree spirits, gnomes, rock beings and the guardians of these kingdoms and also the spirits of the elements—earth, water, fire and air.

Q. *Is their purpose to develop Nature?*

A. Anything to do with Nature is their purpose. Interestingly, Cherub Angel forms look very different than Nature spirits, but they are very similar vibrationally to that kingdom. They would have a different job to do than, let's say, a fairy would. They unify kingdoms in that they bridge the Nature Kingdom to the Angelic world. They're not Nature spirits, but they work with Nature. They serve as connectors between worlds. They oversee and work with the Kingdom of Nature, but their light is different. Nature needs Angel light as well as sunlight to function properly.

Q. *Do Cherub Angels protect the Earth?*

A. They do whatever job needs to be done to keep the Kingdoms of Nature in order. They could be in the forest with the trees or in the water. They could help fish or work closely with amphibians, water creatures or birds. I don't see them working very much with humans in this way. There are many factors that go into keeping the Earth in order—Cherubs play a part in this process.

Q. *Why can't I see more Angels?*

A. You could see them if you meditate on them. I feel it in my solar plexus and I smell flowers when Angels are around—lilies and roses, specifically.

Q. *Why do mainstream religions fear us calling on Angels?*

A. They are very aware of demons and they are generally concerned that people will leave an opening through which they could be possessed. They are concerned about us opening ourselves up to Realms about which we know nothing.

* * *

Q. *What do Angels want from us?*

A. They want us to pay attention! They want us to establish a relationship with them. Everyone's own Guardian Angel has incredible powers of discernment. If we would get close to our own Angel, we'd know our own powers of discernment, which are vitally important now. Many of us lack the ability to discern who's talking to us and how to discern negative energies from positive ones. I'm hearing, "We could avoid tripping ourselves up," if we had greater powers of personal discernment.

Angels also want us to fulfill our contracts. I feel frustration from them because they want us to grow, but we entertain too many negative thoughts and we don't perform to the best of our abilities due to vulnerable parts of ourselves.

Q. *If you're constantly negative, where is your Guardian Angel when it seems the demons are winning?*

A. In terms of the type of power demons have, it's an illusion that they are winning. They can make a person feel lost or cause misery, which leaves a person unable to make good choices. So yes, they can wreak havoc in your life and they can actually ruin your life, but only because you've chosen at some point to listen more to the negative than the positive.

Your Angels are saying,

"We're your strength. If you're down in the depths of despair, you need to call on us for strength."

If you can't think of a positive thought, just say,

"I need strength. Help."

Meet yourself where you are. Don't give yourself some lofty goal if you know you're in a black hole and you need to be able to have some peace of mind. Say, "I need peace of mind *right now*."

Demons play with your mind, but ultimately, you're the one who has to choose to heal whatever is underneath your mind or emotions. You still have free will to ask for help. Source is saying that the direction of your life is up to you.

There are many times when you have to fight. I can remember one of my dark nights when I felt that none of my guidance was there. I kept asking, "Where are you?" No answer. This went on for a couple years. I felt nothing—no help to the point where I thought I must be really bad. I felt abandoned. I thought I must have really gone off my path because none of my Guides were showing up. They weren't helping me.

It took me two and a half years before I got an answer—which was that they were quiet because it was time for me to become more masterful. This meant they wanted me to become more of my own self-sovereign being. There's a point when Source says, "Okay, it's time to grow up. You need to become a more conscious, discerning being who can create."

In your case with the negativity you are experiencing, you can also call on the Immortal Master Babaji for help in releasing any dark energies that might be attached to you.

Q. *Do we ever outgrow our Guides?*

A. Yes, but this doesn't mean that you won't have another type of Guide come in and take you to a higher level. When people get through some of their hardest challenges by sheer perseverance on their own, their lives can change drastically. Think of it in terms of maturity. Each of us is being asked to become our own creator. This implies that the dependency we have on higher beings to look out for us and save us will have to go as we become more self-realized. When your spirit is ready, you will be guided to grow up and become a more conscious manifester.

We are each born with powers of manifestation. There comes a point when we have to examine our own consciousness, look into our own issues and see how our perceptions and beliefs are creating our experiences. We are asked to undo our own belief structures and build new ones that are positive and beneficial to ourselves and to all humankind. Ultimately, as a sovereign spirit, we're the ones who are responsible for ourselves. Guides will help us and then the time comes when they say, "Okay. You've come to this place. Now the next step is to grow further." They will step aside and be silent so you can grow on your own, much as parents who step back to allow their children to grow. We may have fear or think we're not ready. We're being asked to stand up and walk up the mountain. We can do it! There is always help on every level to God Realization. Even though there are times when our Guides step back, we can still ask for peace instead of conflict and we will receive it. Here is the point—as we go through dark times, our maturing process may be to practice choosing peace over conflict, mastery over the belief in victimization. We may be being asked to decide which side of the fence we're going to energize for ourselves. Deciding for peace when you're filled with inner conflict and fear is a huge victory for the soul.

When I say there is always help, I mean encouragement and love is *always* sent while we are going through challenges. The drawing back from our Guides happens during this time because it is a time of choosing in our soul growth. The choices we make determine the growth.

Q. *Is there a place where channelled information is valuable as guidance? I have a friend who claims to channel The Pleiadians and I find the information very valuable.*

A. Source is saying higher beings do not channel through anyone. By 'channeling' I mean when a spirit talks *through* a person who in a trance state, or when the spirit uses the channel's body and voice to deliver messages.

I am distinguishing this from telepathic communication in which the channel is receiving messages while conscious. This is the appropriate form of channeling. Source has always said a higher being has no need to use another person's body to speak. Why would it need it to get a message across in that way? In fact, a higher being is careful about *not* using a person's body.

The Pleiadian world is very scientific and they have given brilliant technological advancements and healing methods, but we've also had some negative technology come from them as well. Positive Pleiadians may spend time *talking to* (not through) people who are going to promote the evolution of the Earth and its species in some way. If this is the case with your friend, that's great. It could also be that he/she was once a Pleiadian and it is his/her own Pleiadian self coming through.

Higher beings impart inspiration or genius. High frequency information comes through telepathically or through knowing.

Participant: "I like that we are here asking questions about Angels and Archangels, which heretofore would have been very entrenched in our religious upbringing. We're asking, "Is it valid to believe in this?" The very fact that we're asking these questions at all is making us choose, which is where, if I understand correctly, Source wants us to go. It wants us to make our own choices based on our knowledge, our information, our growth and our level of maturity."

Aingeal: "Yes, that's it. What I'm hearing about self-mastery isn't that our life is always rosy. It's about how we *respond* to life. Can we respond without freaking out? Are we paralyzed with fear if something happens? Are we connected enough to receive an inspiring answer?

Let's say something totally out of the blue happens, something we've never had to deal with before, something we have no training in. When we're connected to our Inner Self we'll receive information on how to solve the problem. We'll receive the solution because we've asked for it. We'll be able to respond to any situation without feeling powerless.

Achieving higher levels of self-mastery doesn't mean that we never go through a hard time or are never tested. In fact, sometimes the next level could require something difficult to go through. Even if we think we've grown past something, we'll be presented with it again in the future to make sure we've healed what we think we've healed. It isn't because anyone is attacking us—it's because this is how we measure our progress. This is the tempering process that we go through on our ascent.

Q. *I've heard that if we haven't overcome something in a previous life, it will present itself again in a different life. If we can't remember our lifetimes, how do we know what to heal?*

A. You actually don't have to know what's happened in past lives. All you have to know is what's happening in your life *now*. If a situation in your current life is similar to a situation in a past life experience, you're still in the same place in the present.

It's always about, *What are we going to do with it?* What do we need to choose, release, forgive, learn, or overcome? There are times when we'll be shown one of our other lives if there is something in it we need to know. It can be a spontaneous remembering in a flash. But if that isn't happening, carry on with the task at hand. The reality that you're experiencing *now* will tell you what your issues are. Do you like what you're experiencing? Do the same things show up over and over again? It doesn't matter where they came from; it only matters what you do with them and how you can grow from them. Can you transform a pattern if it's something you don't like? Will it take courage, change, forgiveness, purification or releasing? At other times, we get help from our Inner guidance if it will benefit us to know where the pattern originated from.

It might be tempting to associate transforming patterns with learning lessons, but the energy behind them is very different. Lessons imply something that is given us from an outside source—a test in which we can pass or fail.

Lessons imply a training or going through a challenge or hardship in order to learn something. Patterns however, are things inside us that are there because they've been passed down or the result of our own chronic choices and decisions. We can keep repeating the same pattern forever and no one will be there to tell us we can't. There is no authority telling us we have to learn something. We will eventually want to change because we will get tired of the same experience. In this way, we cause our own awakening. A Guide helps us see what the pattern is.

I mentioned the spirit/soul complex wants to achieve *victories*. Victories are the making of a higher choice when presented with a lesser one. It is when a challenge is met with courage and the choosing of a higher virtue. These are victories. They are evidence the person is becoming more aware of God consciousness. They understand that what they choose and decide makes an impact on themselves and the world for good or ill.

My last partner before I met Ahonu, committed suicide. I knew him for eight years as a friend and I knew he suffered from depression. He had been suicidal many times, but I didn't see it coming this time. Because I never saw it coming, I went back to our cabin where it happened six months later because I wanted to know, *What did I miss? I must have missed something*. I asked my Guides to show me what I had missed. I was put in touch with my partners emotions so I could feel and think what he was feeling and thinking at the time. I felt the degree of his pain, his inner torment, his thoughts, his horrible sadness. I don't want to miss something like that ever again. If I ever come across anyone who is like that in my future, I want to be able to know, so I can possibly do something different. I am saying this with the awareness that each person has the right to their choices, but presenting other options to them might also be helpful.

Although the entire event was devastating for me and for everyone who knew and loved him, I was able to understand it with more maturity and centeredness than I would have been able to do in years prior. I could see it spiritually and look at it from a different perspective.

I wanted more awareness about the entire event and went back to the cabin two more times since to gather anything more I could realize from that time in my life. Each visit gave me more awareness, which helped me with my own healing, but also in understanding others who feel this way. I had dreams about my partner for a long time afterwards, seeing the different stages he was going through in spirit and the progress he was making. There was no 'punishment' regarding his suicide, no abandonment or being cast out. He had his life review just as we all will and he chose to contemplate his choices and decisions in spirit. When a person is in spirit, they are still presented with choices and decisions which affect their own further awakening to God realization. We don't ever escape ourselves whether in the body or out.

Let me tell you a story. Last week there was a woman at our meeting who had to take her mother into the emergency room at a hospital in Dublin. Apparently, the negativity in this particular hospital is horrendous from what people say. The woman was affected by this negativity the minute she walked into the emergency room. There was a man in the waiting room who was staring at her with what she felt was evil intent. She felt she was being disarmed by this man's negativity. Severe panic and fear went through her. She did everything she knew for protection and felt that none of it was working. Then, thankfully, another man started a conversation with her which broke the negative energy. That could have been her Guardian Angel's way of helping her in that moment. Even when telling us the story, she was still affected by it and was crying.

In a situation like this, watch your own fear in the moment. Try to become an observer. Take stock in the moment and observe yourself feeling fear, terror or panic. Watch the scene, watch your fear. Ask yourself, "What is this fear really about?" Feel it as deeply as you can and you will locate what is being triggered in you. This way, you do not run from the fear but instead, receive information from it, understand it and be with it. This process will cause the fear to move through you and dissolve.

You can also make a different choice in these moments such as declaring, "I choose peace instead of this!" (from *A Course In Miracles* https://acim.org)

There is evil floating around and it's obvious that there are entities afoot. Is this the collective dark history and shadows of ourselves coming out to be purified as greater light comes in?

I had a series of dreams when I was in my thirties and forties in which I was confronted by evil energies. I consider those confrontations spiritual challenges for awakening. In one dream, I was in an older house in which we had lived some years back. I was going up the stairs to the attic. (Going *up* stairs is usually a symbol of ascent in a dream to a higher level, whereas going *down* stairs indicates a decent into the subconscious or unconscious).

As I climbed these stairs in the dream, three evil beings suddenly appeared to block my way. I knew they were called 'The Bishops of Evil'. They were tall and were an ugly, putrid green color. The energy coming from them was menacing and I was paralyzed with fear. They were very threatening as I looked up at them and I felt very little and powerless in comparison. Then I heard the same voice I had heard in another dream say, "There's only one God." As soon as I heard that, the evil beings vanished. What I awakened to from that experience is that Source is the only Truth and anything else that appears to be different or unloving is an illusion. I've had to be reminded of that over and over throughout my spiritual journey.

In conclusion, the important thing to realize is that we have help and protection from so many things. We are not alone. We can become much more conscious of our own Guardian Angel and our own higher aspects. As much as we are given Guides, Mentors and a Guardian Angel, it is still Sources's intention that we rise up into our own I AM Presence and be a force for good. We are not meant to stay dependent like children, but become our God Self incarnate. This goal is what all true guidance is about.

Chapter Seven

Our Light Bodies

Our Light Bodies

Aingeal: "Most people are aware we have an aura around our bodies that can be photographed and seen as a moving and colorful array of light that shifts and changes in each moment. What may not be as familiar to people is our *light bodies*, which extend farther than the aura and encompass much more than our physical bodies. Today, we explore these light bodies from Source's point of view. As I'm said the opening prayer, a brilliant emerald-green light was present, as well as a very strange white vortex of light that looked like a tunnel leading into infinity."

Q. *What is Source's definition of 'lightbody'?*

A. I see beautiful striations of light that appear as woven patterns encompassing us. These patterns of light are not only emanating *from* us, they are *surrounding* us as well. We are immersed in this intricate pattern, or network of light, which is everywhere. I also hear the vibrations of this network which sound like continuous hums or pulses of sound with varying tones. This is an interrelated network of light that connects all things together. We are made up of it, but we don't *cause* the rest of the network to be what it is.

'Lighbodies' appear as concentrated networks of light in and of themselves. I wish everyone could see this picture! There are these beautiful striations of light that extend throughout all Creation and when you come to a particular life form, it is a *concentrated* or *focused* network of light, giving it an appearance of definition and solidity. I see our bodies as beautiful concentrations of light.

Q. *What is the purpose of these 'lightbodies'?*

A. They are what you are made of. They are points of Creation that allow for particular forms of expression. Every life form is made up of light and sound and has its own unique combination of light strands. Each one is having its own unique experience in the creative field. The purpose of 'light bodies', therefore, is to allow you to experience life in a myriad of ways, to become aware of the Creator and your creative potential and to become a conscious creator yourself.

Your ability to become aware is also in the original design of light and sound. It is easy to see that life forms are at varying degrees of awareness. Some could be considered *inert*, meaning that their ability to become aware is very limited. Others could be very advanced in awareness. The particular arrangement of light and sound as it coalesces into form determines its potential for awareness. The more potential for awareness a life form has, the more knowledge and understanding it can gain in its experience. Source is saying that the purpose of life is to enjoy life and experience it while becoming aware of the vastness, power, love and infinite potential of Creation. We should be looking at Creation as a playground designed for our enjoyment. Becoming aware of Source enables us to understand the Love that is the basis of reality. Only when we understand love will our creations be harmless and ecstatic. Our lightbody's allow us to coalesce into form for this purpose. We can become many forms, not just human. Each form coalesces for a limited time, then unravels and becomes a new form at another time or place.

Q. *Can we control how light and sound coalesce into form?*

A. As you become more and more aware, you begin to understand how to mold light and sound, causing them to come together and coalesce into shapes and forms, which then unravel and become striations of light once again.

This is an ongoing process and we can focus our attention so as to communicate with these strands and intend them to come together in particular forms or experiences. We are in a sea of interwoven sound and light particles. You can call them to you and mold them. So yes, you can play with these striations. They hold the intelligence of Source and they know how to rearrange themselves according to the focused attention of consciousness.

It would be good to begin exploring this process through your own body by focusing on yourself and looking at your own particular light and sound arrangement that you call your body. If there are things you'd like to change about it, you could begin to communicate with your lightbody and give it a new image to form. Everything about you—your organs, glands, bones, blood and skin—is made of light and sound. All of it can be altered and rearranged, once you know you have the power to work with yourself in this way. You can become your own scientist.

Regarding *control* over light and sound, Source would rather that we use the word '*play*', as it more accurately describes the joy of the creative process. Obviously, your level of awareness and the quality of your consciousness has much to do with your ability to mold light and sound to affect your own body.

Q. *How do we expand our awareness of our lightbody's?*

A. This conversation is already expanding your awareness of them. You can sit down, close your eyes and focus inward. Put your attention and intention on your lightbody and see if you can see it. It should appear as a myriad of glowing and sparkling light strands. You should be able to see the intricate patterns that are woven to make up your body. There will be points of light that are distinct from the woven patterns as they crisscross and intersect one another. Realize that you can communicate with your light body and ask it to show you areas that may need reinforcement or repair, or it can simply show you its condition via a feeling or by drawing your attention to a particular area of your body.

As you scan yourself thoroughly and you look at all parts of your body and its systems, you can mold or alter specific areas that need attention or change.

You can change the patterns that you see to *mean* something new and different. Consider that the particular patterns in your body have come together by more than a few causes. One cause is the genetic pattern you inherited from your parents; another is the pastlife imprints that you bring forward into this life and another is your collection of beliefs and feelings about yourself, your life, this reality, *etc*.

To play with and change your patterns, you first need to become aware of what those patterns are. While you scan your own body and see the patterns that make up your identity, see if you can get a *feeling* of what those patterns are composed of. Do you like them? Are they patterns you'd like to keep or do they feel heavy and inhibiting to you?

Once you make an assessment of yourself, you can then go in with your consciousness and give those patterns a different direction. It is as simple as telling your light and sound patterns how you would like them to rearrange themselves in your body and life. Make this a weekly practice and record your findings and any results you notice in a notebook. If you are doing this diligently, you will begin to see the expanse of yourself and your connection to the Universe of light and sound. This will greatly contribute to your self awareness and it will reveal your relationship to all of life. Your perceptions of yourself and the world around you will change greatly as you begin to realize what unlimited potential you have.

Source is telling us that this discipline is not to be used to manipulate any other person into doing your bidding.

There is really nothing solid about us. In fact, the entire Universe is simply an array of light and sound that arranges itself in a wide variety of appearances. This network is pliable and it responds to our conscious intentions. We are continually *forming* our quality without using our consciousness.

Now that we are conscious of our ability to change our own structure, we can move into another level of self-mastery.

Q. *Is our sound body different from our lightbody?*

A. When you mention sound, I see this brilliantly vibrating blue light. It has a bit of aqua-green color to it, but it is predominantly blue and I can feel its vibration. We do have a part of us that is a sound body and it is music. The sound body is made up of musical tones and vibrations. Sound and light interrelate to create form. Both bodies seem to have been created simultaneously. I do not see either sound or light coming first and causing the other; rather they seem to have come from the same original idea of Creation at the same time. You can't have one without the other—each is part of the other.

Sound, in particular is how a shape or geometry comes into being, because there's a series of harmonics that go into the manifestation of forms. Sound is something that has coalesced. because of a particular pattern of light. As a pattern of light starts to define itself, it begins to vibrate which creates sound tone frequencies.

What I find interesting with what is being presented, is that the human shape coalesces into a musical *orchestra*. If we could see and hear our own light patterns, we could hear our own songs which we each have depending upon the makeup of our particular light and sound bodies. I find this incredibly fascinating because if we were to begin disciplining ourselves and go within, we could hear the sounds of our organs, bones, blood, *etc*. Every life form has its own song as sound is a vibratory field that is filled with musical notes, tones, hums and harmonies. Our lightbody and sound body are interrelated.

The closest I've come to this is when my spiritual activations allow me to hear my cells hum and feel my whole body vibrate, which I hear and feel from within. Another time when I've heard my own sounds is when I've gone into a flotation tank, which is completely soundproof and lightproof to the outside. You float in a bath of Epsom salts and water in complete darkness. When I was in this tank, it was so quiet that I began to hear my cells hum. It is a wonderful experience.

Source is saying that the area of sound technology is something we have not yet explored to a wide degree. The ancients had a greater knowledge of sound and its ability to assemble and disassemble matter. The mineral kingdom has many sound tones held within it, which is how large stones could be moved by sound technology. It is also why the use of stone in buildings and structures provides unique healing energies and uplifting feelings.

The reason why it is important to *'Know Thyself'* is because we will all be pleasantly surprised to discover the inner workings of our own nature! Not only can we work with our own particular form and shape, but we can expand it, travel on waves of light with it and experiment with it.

Q. *Were the Lemurian's light beings?*

A. Yes, the Lemurian's were standing columnar waves of light, color and sound. The Lemurian's were never as densely physical as we are now. They were on this planet at a time when the Earth herself was not this dense.

Q. *A Course in Miracles mentions the 'Son of God' and to me, the 'Son of God' and the Sun seem to be the same. Are they the same?*

A. There are many levels to this answer, but it is believed that as we achieve more awareness and God-realization, each of us can become an actual *sun*—not the Sun we see in our sky, but a radiating ball of light that becomes another *source* of life. Because we are not yet at this level, we need the external Sun to provide a source of light for us while we are in this dimension. We are nourished by it; it causes life to grow here and many of us need more Vitamin D, which comes from the Sun.

However, as we become masters, we become more radiant from *within* and no longer need an external Sun. You can notice this when you are around highly evolved people—you feel good around them and you feel stronger and more positive because they have evolved to a place where they hold much light and love. This force can heal you automatically. You can also notice the reverse when you encounter a very dark or negative person who exudes a power that draws you in or drains your energy because the negative person is *taking* your light, whereas someone who is highly evolved is *giving* you light.

Here's a story:

"A few years back a woman came to me for a reading. She was interested in looking into the Akashic Records to see where many famous deceased people had gone. She wanted to know what they were doing in their spirit forms. She asked about 30 famous people, one of whom was Gandhi. In looking at him, I found that he was the only one of the 30 who had become a violet ball of light.

So, the *Son* of God is what each of us *is*, and a *Sun*, or ball of light, is the potential that each of us can become."

Q. *What other techniques will help us see our 'lightbody's?*

A. Seeing your 'lightbody' is like developing your psychic abilities. The 'lightbody' is here right now. Our psychic sight as it has been, has not developed to see finer levels of light and sound. We can see the *effects* of light and sound such as when sand is vibrated and begins to take on varying geometrical shapes depending upon the vibration induced, but we do not normally *see* light and sound as they coalesce into form. One of the best ways to develop your psychic ability or inner sight is simply to focus *inward* daily for at least 10 to 15 minutes as mentioned earlier. It is the practice of giving attention to a specific goal that brings success. This practice is easy.

You can focus inward sitting up or lying down, lying on the beach or relaxing in a tub— just about anywhere. Close your eyes and focus within with an intention to see, hear and learn about your 'lightbody'. If you practice this three or four times a week, you should begin to see not only your own lightbody, but the lightbody in all its forms. You will begin to develop your inner sight which will allow you to see at finer levels. Becoming psychic is like developing a muscle—in this case your pineal gland. As you practice your inner focus you exercise this gland, which begins to become activated. The more you use it, the more it develops.

Q. *Is my lightbody the same shape as my physical body?*

A. I'm not seeing a distinction between your physical form and your lightbody. Your physical form is *composed* of your lighbody and your aura is an *emanation* coming from your body. We have to think differently about how we see ourselves. What we see as our physical body is really our lightbody that has coalesced into a particular shape and form. Our physical body is the shape of our lightbody because it is made of our lightbody. The only reason our bodies seem to stay a certain way is because our consciousness hasn't changed in its core beliefs about the body, its limits and the reality of 3D.

The aura is an *emanation* from your body and it changes in its appearance depending upon the condition of your body and consciousness. I'm not seeing the aura *as* the 'lightbody'—rather, it is an *emanation* from your lightbody/physical body.

When I lived in Chicago, I would often get my auric photo taken and for many years it showed the same colors—white, violet and blue. It wasn't until I began to change my body and incorporate some new spiritual techniques that my aura also changed color. It began to take on bright yellows, greens and pinks, showing me that I was becoming more vibrant in my physical self, something I greatly needed at the time.

The aura is a result of the condition of the physical/lightbody. Kirlian photography of leaves, plants and human body parts also show light emanating from them. The emanation of light from fingers does not *cause* the fingers, but rather it shows the frequency of light coming off the fingers The aura is the discharge coming from the object, like the rays of light that come off the Sun are not the Sun itself, but are emanations from it.

Q. *Do creatures, plants, minerals or animals have 'lightbody's'?*

A. Yes. Source is saying that everything is composed of light and sound. Each form has its own unique woven pattern that makes it what it is. Some may think that a rock doesn't have much light in it, seeing as it is so compact. However, it may have more *sound* in it because of its density. It is still composed of both light and sound, but its woven pattern would be different than that from another form, like a tree, for example. It's the same principle for all forms that we see, which is one of the wonderful aspects of the diversity of which we are a part. Humans can be consciously aware of their own composition and they can mold and change their own patterns as well as those of other life forms with their consciousness.

Think of the awakening consciousness in people and all the healing modalities that have come on board in the last few decades. These healing modalities provide a supply of light and sound to us through the practitioner providing healing on various levels. As advanced as all this is becoming, it is still not the same as going within and learning to change our own biology. The incredible potential of knowing ourselves by going within is enormous. Not only that, but the discoveries we may encounter along the way can be the greatest adventures we've ever had. Throughout this second book in the series, Source has repeatedly encouraged us to go within and not measure ourselves through the outer world. It only takes 15-30 minutes a day for you to begin to change the entire structure of your world. The possibilities are endless!

If you feel you are not ready to do this, the use of energy practitioners and healing techniques can still be of great benefit to you and may help activate your higher centers.

Q. *Do healing devices like light tables or the machines that shine light onto the body through colors and crystals really work?*

A. Yes, they provide color frequencies which are nourishing and regenerative. Colors affect your light/physical body since light is composed of colors as we discussed earlier. Putting more color into your body changes your light pattern depending upon the particular colors chosen. Colors change hormones and chemicals in the body, so it's important to know whether a person needs certain colors or has too much of a certain color. If you have a deficiency in a particular color, it will improve your health to add that color. If you have too much of a certain color, adding more may make you ill.

Color therapy is a very powerful modality in and of itself, so yes, the devices you mention above can have a positive effect. When you receive a needed color or light, you can repair at every level. Healing energy can help heal physical conditions but it can also change your emotional state and your perceptions. The key for lasting change is to hold that new emotion or perception so you don't revert back to a previous pattern.

Q. *Are we moving toward 'lightbody ascension'?*

A. Source told us we have the *potential* for it. 'Lightbody ascension' is when you come into full recognition of yourself as a lightbody and you master the patterns of your lightbody and the physical world. Ascension is when you understand that densification of the body and form are perceptions in our consciousness. When you work with and change the patterns of light and sound, you are no longer bound by the physics of this world—you've gone beyond the belief that the physical world is solid and unmovable.

You begin to experience yourself as a being of light and demonstrate your ability to alter things in this world. Ascended beings come to know themselves on levels that go far beyond the physical. We can go as far as we can into lightbody ascension, but it requires we master the ability to unravel ourselves and turn our bodies back into light any time we choose. Lightbody ascension is not some magical occurrence that will happen *to* us on a particular date or through any specific event. What *has* been occurring, however, is an increase of light from the Cosmos which has been activating the light patterns of which we are made, thus increasing our awareness.

Q. *Is death a part of ascension?*

A. Death is *not* part of ascension—it is the result of our consciousness. Ascension is the spirit releasing the belief in death and demonstrating this through its ability to move in and out of the physical body at will. An ascended being is not affected by anything it does not want to be affected by. An ascended being takes its body into light and does not go through the death process that we do. The biggest challenge in working with our lightbody's, as stated earlier, is undoing many of our false perceptions concerning our physicality and the physical world.

In physical death, your spirit essence leaves your body and is still only at the level of its own consciousness. I'm not talking about the lightbody right now, which is a woven pattern of light that forms your physicality. Your spirit is your God essence that is growing and evolving to become God-realized. When we die, we die at the level of our consciousness or spirit development, which is why spirits go to many different planes of existence after death. What or who a spirit sees when it dies depends upon their beliefs and their consciousness. The saying "In my Father's house are many mansions" indicates the many levels and planes of existence in the spirit world. Therefore, it is not a given that when you die you automatically ascend. Ascension is the mastery of your spiritual nature and your place in the Universe.

Q. *Is Earth moving into her lightbody ascension?*

A. I hear Earth saying she is still predominantly affected by Cosmic forces. Planets are all affected by each other and by Cosmic forces. What happens on one planet affects all others, *etc.* They are in a vast interrelationship with each other in their particular solar system. The light patterns that we call planets coalesce as a particular solar system. When we speak about different forms being able to cause changes in their own patterns, planets seem to be dependent on one another in part for their evolution. The Earth is saying that she cannot change herself the way we can change ourselves. She can have her own intention for her evolution, but that evolution is still interconnected to the other planets in this Solar System. Our Solar System with all its members, including planets, stars, novae and quasars, Sun and Moon and cycles, are all interconnected with one another. Since most planets are made of rock and minerals, their ability to consciously change or undo their own patterning is limited. Earth is saying that she cannot be an independent thinker and decider of her own makeup. She is still an interdependent member with the other members of the Solar System.

On one level, we could say that the same is true of us in that we are all connected to one another. However, we can advance in our awareness and consciousness by what we do with our own thoughts and decisions. We can become free of established paradigms by the activation of the God nature within us. We can change our form with our consciousness.

So, when you ask whether the Earth is heading toward her lightbody ascension, I hear her saying that she isn't able to yet because of what is happening throughout the Solar System. On the other hand, what we do here as humans does collectively affect the entire Solar System and its planets. We *do* have a hand in how other planets evolve. The Earth herself, as powerful as she is with her forces of Nature, is still under the collective evolution of the Solar System.

Source really wants us to hear this because our consciousness can do so many things. If we decide that we do not want to go within and learn about our true nature or experiment with our Lightbody's, Chakras or Kundalini, we will remain like the Earth —subject to the forces outside of ourselves that act upon us seemingly without our will or consent. We will be affected by all the other consciousness around us and everything that happens as a result. We will be carried along on a particular evolutionary track, completely dependent upon the *quality* of the masses.

Of course, we have a right to stay exactly as we are without ever going within. There is no judgment in Source. What Source is saying however, is that we have a consciousness that is becoming more aware and so our possibilities are unlimited. If you take on an inner discipline, you will be one who can affect the quality of life in this Solar System in a very positive way. You can do what you want. You can stay in the evolutionary cycle of time, space and Cosmic forces or you can gain your freedom from all perceived limitations. Every person who gains his/her freedom contributes to that potential for everyone.

If we stay at the evolutionary cycle and remain predominantly unconscious, we will either eventually evolve and progress further or we will digress into deeper unconsciousness.

Other solar systems have their own sets of patterns with their own planets and they would be considered dependent upon one another in their system.

Q. *Does what we eat, where we live or the circumstances we find ourselves in, affect our lightbody's?*

A. Yes, because the quality of light, sound and color in food either strengthens or weakens your lightbody pattern. Let's talk about the difference between *dead* food and *live* food. A piece of white bread, for example, made from genetically modified seeds that have been ground down with most of their nutrients and fiber stripped away, will not have many nutrients in it. It will be missing enzymes, minerals, amino acids and vitamins. It will have very little light and sound to offer the consumer. If we compare this to eating edible flowers or fresh vegetables and fruits that have been grown organically without genetically modified seeds and not sprayed with pesticides and fungicides, you will have a food that is happy and filled with light and sound particles. This would have much to offer the consumer. Notice, I am using the word *consumer*. We are answering this question from the point of view of someone with the consciousness who still needs to eat to stay alive in this dimension. Of course, this is 99.99% of the population! We are not talking about someone who has mastered the physical world and no longer needs to consume other life forms to survive.

As for how *places* affect our light bodies, we can use the same analogy as we did with different types of food. Every place carries its own unique vibration and grid pattern. Some places uplift and support your light body and other places weaken it. Remember, there is a bigger picture. The dominant thing that affects you is your state of consciousness. We are talking about different states of awareness when answering this question. All states of awareness from the lowest to the highest are accepted in Source.

To put things in the outer world in perspective, let's consider some yogis who have been known to consume nothing but sugar, tobacco and coffee. There are other stories of yogis who have taken many drugs, none of which affected them in the slightest. These yogis remained healthy and strong and lived to old ages because they found another world within themselves that was not dependent upon externals to be healthy.

Some people have been known to live only on sunlight or the prana in the atmosphere. These examples are extreme of course, but they show the varying levels of consciousness that can be achieved. Until we go within to know ourselves and master ourselves, we will still be affected by many external things.

Q. *Does the radiation used in cancer treatments or from nuclear accidents affect our body's light strands?*

A. We can apply the answer above to this question, but let's see what Source has to say about radiation. Sometimes radiation promotes the growth of new life forms and sometimes it destroys existing ones. It has the potential to evolve a species, while in others it creates distortions. It can change plant and animal life by evolving it forward, but it can also mutate or destroy species.

The effect radiation has on a particular lifeform has everything to do with how its light patterns are configured. Radiation vibrates at a faster frequency than what is considered normal in our dimension—it's why a lifeform will either use radiation to further itself or it will be destroyed by it.

If our frequency could handle the frequency of radiation, it would have no harmful effect on us. We have been receiving increased radiation from the Sun in recent years, which has awakened many of us, but has also resulted in sickness and death for others. We are in a great time of change with incredible potential for both evolution and destruction. Whether a life form evolves or is destroyed depends upon its personal condition, which is why some people get well from having radiation treatments for cancer and some people die from it.

In conclusion, consider getting together in groups to focus inward on your lightbody's and become your own scientists. It would be a rewarding project!

Chapter Eight

Love

Love

Q. *What is Source's definition of Love?*

A. Love is the field of all expression where everything *is* and is allowed to be expressed. It is a dynamic, alive field where anything is possible. It is the desire and intention of Source that life *be* and it is the relationship of all life to all life. It accepts what is expressed within it, whether that expression be for good or ill. It upholds the highest creative possibility and integrity and can't be destroyed. Love says "Yes!" to whatever you desire in that it is a dynamic, creative field. Love holds all things in high esteem and promotes expression in greater and greater measures. It does not judge. It is forever responsive to our thoughts and desires.

Q. *What are Love's qualities?*

A. Love is free because there is no judgment within it. It is a dynamic field in the sense that it *responds* to everything, even though it doesn't judge what it's responding to. Its response is to allow. Love is innocent in its allowance, meaning it is completely harmless in its intent. It's the field where all possibilities exist and can be expressed and actualized. It is a dynamic and creative field. Love never ends or dies. It's not an energy—rather, it is the creative life force itself and everything in existence is composed of its essence. It is the will and intention of God Source, which is that life exist and express itself.

Imagine looking up into the Universe and watching the field of all possibilities, knowing that everything and anything is possible, accepted and allowed.

Imagine that there are no limits to this Creation. Imagine yourself as a life form that is formed from Love's essence, that is completely loved and accepted, who has permission to express itself as it desires without limitation. Imagine that there are no boundaries to life. Imagine a quality of life that upholds your highest possible expressions and also allows your lowest. Imagine a Presence that is ever patient because it allows until you decide differently. Imagine never being judged; imagine only being welcomed.

Q. *Is there an opposite to Love?*

A. No. Within this field of Love, you can express however you wish. Some people express in an unloving way, yet in the field of Love, all is allowed. Unloving expressions are not Loves opposite because the field of Love cannot be damaged in any way. I know many of us have experienced very tragic things, but Love is still intact and its benign presence can be felt through any adversity. Love is not the *cause* of tragedy or suffering—it is our choices that cause suffering. Still, Love allows all our choices until we are ready to make higher ones. In this regard, how much of Love we can feel or experience is determined by the quality of our choices. As our choices become more and more loving in their nature, we can then feel more of Love's presence because 'like attracts to itself, that which it is'.

There is no opposite to Love because Love is all encompassing. It is the original template from God Source and it is the Truth that never changes. It is an Absolute Truth—a constant and the blueprint behind all life. Without it, life would not be. Choices that are unloving in their motive have their consequences as a result of the Law of Cause and Effect. Love is a field that allows for all expressions and choices—it doesn't judge them and cannot be destroyed by them. This is why it has no opposite.

Q. *How present is Love in our world?*

A. Love is completely present in our world, but the ability to feel and actualize its Presence and experience its power is determined by our own choices and beliefs. The proportion of Love in our world is unlimited, but the *experiencing* of It in our world is determined by the quality of our decisions and beliefs and how much of pure Love we can accept.

Q. *What's the relationship between Love and hate?*

A. There is no relationship between Love and hate. Love *is*. We didn't say that Love is the expression of everything—we said that Love *allows* the expression of everything.

Q. *Are they opposites?*

A. No, they are not opposites because Love has no opposite. To think that it does is part of the illusion we're under. We think because of the limits of our polarity perception, that if you have Love, it has to have an opposite. This is not so.

We try to down-step the different experiences we have and put them in categories so we can make sense of our world. Source is saying that evil, or hatred can't come close to what Love is. Evil and hatred are the formations that result from choices that are made and beliefs that we hold. Love *allows* for those expressions, but it clearly does not create them. They have no comparison to Love. There are no similarities because evil and hatred's perceived power and reality is based on illusions held in the mind. It's the difference between real and unreal.

Love is *real*, meaning it is forever and unlimited in its qualities and power. Evil or hatred is finite and limited in its power. This is because Love is the life force of Creation and simply *is*, whereas negative expressions come from beliefs, which are illusory and have no life force of their own except for what an individual gives them.

They can seem to take on very potent and powerful expressions, as indeed the mind is very powerful. However, negative expressions do not carry true lifeforce energy, therefore they are temporary in their expressions.

Beneath all expressions of hatred or evil is a fear of being unloved or an unawareness of Love's presence. Because of this underlying fear, it appears that we must take or conquer what we need from life. We all have varying degrees of this fear within us. It is always the fear of not being loved or sustained by Love or of feeling unworthy that lies beneath all expressions of hatred or evil.

Still, in this field of Love that I'm seeing, there is no judgment around unloving expressions, even though we judge them here on Earth. The field of Love doesn't put them in any category whatsoever, which is very interesting. The problem with judging things and putting them into categories is that we only make more of them. The minute we label something or make a judgment about its being bad or good, right or wrong, we make more of whatever we're judging. Source's intention is Love, bliss and ecstasy.

Source is *not* saying that good and evil are both expressions of Love, or that they are the same. Even though we're not judging hatred or evil, we're not saying that they're the same as Love. *They are not*. We're saying that Love *allows* all expressions. Source's original intention is only Love, which is a dynamic and creative force. It is non-judgment, unlimited potentiality, freedom of expression, welcoming, acceptance, innocence, harmless causation and unlimited opportunity to realize higher and higher expressions of Itself without end. When we behave counter to that, Love doesn't condemn because it allows it all. Imagine for a moment that you were never told you were bad or wrong. Imagine that there was no incrimination or disapproval, but only acceptance and welcoming. Would you be a different person? Would you look on others differently and behave differently? You would, as you would be transformed by the experience.

Q. *If we have a life review after death, isn't that being judged?*

A. No. What happens is that you see a movie of your life and you experience everything—every action and reaction as the cause and effect of your choices, both high and low. You will experience yourself in a relationship with all life everywhere. Whatever someone else felt by your actions and behaviors will be shown to you as if you were experiencing it yourself. You will see what qualities or lack of quality you have donated to life. You have either contributed to the experiencing and awareness of more Love or you have deterred it. It could be a mixture of both. You will realize that you're partaking of everything and you are in relationship with everything. When you realize this, you will see how important and powerful you are.

For example, let's say that a mass murderer crosses over. The same process or review will be as true for him/her as it is for everyone else. Both the acts of Love and the acts of harm will all be experienced as if the doer was also the receiver. We are shown what effect our beliefs and actions have had on everything, positive as well as negative. We'll be able to see it and experience it all. There is no one waiting at the gate to send you to heaven or hell. You will experience yourself through your own behaviors, actions, victories and failures.

Q. *Then we can get away with a few bad things?*

A. Not really, because you're going to experience what the other person experienced as a result of you—good and not so good. You'll get to know that it's all one relationship with everyone and everything. So, there's no escape or separating yourself from your own cause and effect.

Our perceptions are very interesting because we use our perceptions to separate and put things in categories. We put others in categories by our perceptions of them. We say that things are separate from us and we label things. The truth is that there's no separation between anything or anyone.

Here's another way to explain it: Remember when we were little and we'd have a bubble bath? We'd splash the water and make more bubbles. In this Field of all expression we're all making more bubbles. Whether we know it or not, every time a bubble is made, we experience it on some level of our being. It goes into our cells as knowledge or experience. Each 'bubble' has a unique wavelength because we created it, which means that everyone will know it on some level because we're all immersed in the 'All That Is'. The bubble is in the collective 'soup'. It's like adding another spice—everybody gets to 'taste' what you've added to the Field at some level.

Q. *Surviving concerns me— are those who are more open, accepting and integrated more likely to survive?*

A. Perhaps Love's response to your fear is to show you that you *do* or will survive. It could be survival on this dimension to allay your fears if that will serve your awakening, or it can be you leave this dimension and you see that you still *are*. Remember that we all survive as our spirit selves, whether we stay in a body or not. I know you are concerned with your physical body survival. I can't say that those who are more aware of God Source than others are more likely to survive. Everyone has their own personal life plan going on. It all depends on individual soul contracts. Some may be meant to stay here and some may be meant to leave and that may be determined by their soul contract rather than their frequency.

A Course in Miracles addresses the idea of conflict. It says in order to stop experiencing conflict in our lives we have to give up the *idea* of conflict. The belief in it has to go. So, here we are talking about hatred and evil and we're being asked to choose only Love. It isn't that you don't see evil things happen. Obviously, if someone's behaving in evil ways, it can't be denied and there are those who appear 'soul-less' We're not trying to say that unloving behavior is Love. It isn't. Instead, when you consciously choose to hold yourself to higher and higher standards of Love, you lose interest in judging others. You recognize that beneath the surface, all evil behavior is a call for Love. How do you handle it?

If you have someone who's behaving insanely and criminally, you still have to remove them from society. You can't allow them to continue victimizing others, perpetuating the victim-victimizer game. The loving thing to do is to stop them from continuing to harm. I'm not talking about killing anyone. You can remove someone from society while understanding that all unloving acts are degrees of insanity and calls for Love. If you said, "I love you" to a person committing a crime, it may or may not have an effect on them, depending on the degree of their insanity. They may not be vibrating at a level where they can hear or accept that thought. Obviously, someone behaving in unloving and destructive ways has no self-love, but within your own being, you can know that they are as unconditionally loved by Source as anyone else. At the level of Source, there is no judgment.

The Law of Cause and Effect is still in place as long as there is time. This is the Law of 'like attracts like'. Even so, in your own heart you can know that one brother is all brothers and we can look on a brother with love and harmless intent no matter what the circumstances. You can do this while you lock the jail door, until the one who is behaving insanely chooses Love and lives from Love. This happens when the person is ready—it could take one or many lifetimes. Redemption can happen in an instant. It is not our place to magnify a person's guilt with our thoughts—it is our job to forgive and love, while removing a person from society who is harming others. Again, we are not talking about killing anyone—that is not our place.

In light of the extreme example above, we need to look at our own behavior and thoughts to see how well we are choosing high standards of Love for ourselves and others. We may be causing as much damage with our own unloving thoughts or actions each day towards ourselves or others as a criminal would by an outward action.

Many believe that we need the yin and the yang—the good and the bad. However, I keep hearing Source say, "No. No." Those things that would be considered evil are not equal to Source's Love. The problem is that we believe both good and evil are *real* and we think both are necessary. *Only Love is real.* Evil is based on false perception. It has no self generative power of its own. Many people believe that in order to know Love, you have to experience hate, or in order to know good, you have to experience evil. Source is not agreeing with that. When you encounter Love, it is a full experience in its own right. If you experience evil, you automatically know it is not Love—there is nothing about it that feels loving. Neither is a requirement for the other to be known.

Q. *What is the difference between frequency and vibration?*

A. It's possible to see this might be a polarity. Remember, we are talking about forces of Nature that concern the material Universe. The Earth is more magnetic, therefore its vibration is heavier. As vibration increases, it becomes denser or heavier—more compact or 'physical', not lighter. We're trying to raise our oscillation rate to bring in a higher frequency, or more electricity, thus having *less* vibration, or magnetics. We're trying to fill our Earth bodies with more spiritual consciousness, which is light based or more electrical. Magnetics are vibration, but frequency is oscillation.

When you increase your vibration, you make yourself heavier.
When you increase your frequency, you make yourself lighter.

Our bodies are more carbon based or magnetic because the Earth is more carbon based. However, as our Earth body incorporates more light, its biology becomes more light based, which means that we become more electrical in nature.

Q. *If we are made of Love, why do we feel so bereft of Love?*

A. I just got an image of Santa Claus with a bag of gifts. Source is saying, "We've forgotten that Santa Claus is real and there is no coal coming to us, only good." Every time we judge someone, we feel bereft of Love because we can't judge someone and not feel the consequences of it somewhere in ourselves.

The belief in judgment makes us feel guilty. When we feel guilty, we believe we are not loved and will be punished. We can't feel or be Love if we're judging, which is why we feel bereft of Love. If we didn't believe in judgment and we knew we can't judge and we understood that Source loves everyone the same, we would be in a state of harmlessness and in respect of others. In this state, we would never feel bereft of Love. Love demonstrates its reality when we're ready to welcome it and become it.

Q. *What is the role of Grace in relation to Love?*

A. Grace is an action or quality of Love—it is the blessing that is Love that forgives and returns to the state of innocence. It affirms and confirms that goodness not only exists, but it is also deserved.

When someone's annoying you, bless them instead of judging them. Intend grace for them and allow it to express itself however it can be expressed for that person. Grace is the blessing that comes out of Love. You won't know how it will manifest in a person's life and you don't need to know. You're not being specific and saying, "I'm blessing you because I want you to do this or that." You're blessing them by acknowledging that they are innocent in God's eyes, just as you are, even if they're not behaving like it or don't know it.

Q. *Tell us about loving and forgiving ourselves and others?*

A. Self-forgiveness is necessary for each of us. When we don't forgive ourselves or someone else, we stay in guilt together with them. This means you and they are locked together into an event or a perception where neither can be free. It serves no one to remain in unforgiveness. It does not allow for the experience or the awareness of Love and is not Source's will. Source would prefer we learn from our mistakes and choose more loving expressions in the present and the future rather than stay bogged down in the past.

Q. *Is self-judgment like, I'm too fat, I'm too thin, etc?*

A. Those are surface examples, but it can be much more tragic than that. We cause our own death, our own illness, our own lack and losses. Think about what's beneath this, really. The *belief* in judgment has to go, not just the act of judging or not judging. Judgment is the belief in guilt. As long as you believe in guilt, you will project that belief in victimization upon yourself and out into the world. If you believe in victimization, you can't believe you're loved, that you're made of love or that you reside in a vast field of Love now and always. Further, you won't believe in your own innate goodness, which deserves the best of everything because that's how God Source made you, everyone and everything. The belief in victim/victimizer and Love don't go together.

Surrendering to forgiveness means you are willing to give up all belief in judgment, guilt and victimization. Close your eyes and imagine, just for a minute, that those concepts and words do not exist. Let yourself feel what it feels like that no one ever made you wrong or judged you in any way. Imagine you never judged anyone or yourself. Imagine that you were never guilty.

Instead, when mistakes were made, you were met with loving kindness and compassion and were given more love and grace to make a better choice. Imagine that you were always given another opportunity and another and another.

Imagine that you did the same for others, which is what Love does. It is ever patient and keeps offering opportunities to know and experience greater and greater realizations of Love.

The choice to give up the idea and the belief in guilt, conflict and judgment is always available whenever we are ready. The reason we haven't come to this realization is because we want other people to be guilty so we can feel justified in our grievances. We all do and have done this. There's no way we can know we're loved or experience what real Love is as long as we're doing that. Beneath the surface we'll always have the fear that God will punish us because we know at some level that judging brings its own consequences. But so do all loving actions.

Q. *If I stop being guilty, is it automatically replaced with Love?*

A. Love is what's there and has always been there. You will now be aware of it and feel it more deeply.

Q. *So you don't have to work at Love?*

A. No, Love is what's naturally there when you give up the belief in guilt and judgment. This field of Love has always been there. It has not gone and is not going anywhere. You don't need to work at Love, you need to work at releasing judgment and accepting love as the only reality.

Q. *Do we have to work at forgiveness?*

A. Only if you're not willing to surrender your belief in guilt. Ask Source by saying, "Help me surrender these beliefs." It's only work when you notice how many times judgment surfaces and how many times you have to remind yourself that guilt and judgment are not real.

Q. *So, we don't have to try to love ourselves or others?*

A. No, not when you truly forgive and bless. When you take away the beliefs mentioned above, you are aware of your communion with life at a much deeper level. Your awareness and sensitivity to subtler energies increases. When you're in communion, or communication at these deeper levels, you feel Love's presence more and more. You're no longer interested in judgment. You begin to experience everyone and everything as yourself. You realize that you are good and God's will for you and all life is goodness. You determine how able you are to receive that goodness.

Participant 1: "Communion is such an interesting term."

Participant 2: "Say it very slowly... Comm-union... Come into union. Come into unity. It means we belong."

Participant 3: "Guilt and judgment form a disconnecting, separating energy making me feel alone and deprived."

Aingeal: "Yes, communion is also communication. When people say, I feel disconnected, I would like to be more in tune with everything, or I would like to be more psychic, those are naturally there when you give up the beliefs in guilt and judgment. Your ability to give and receive information from the field of Love is just there.

The things we use judgment for—somebody's fat or thin, unkempt or neat, poor or wealthy, etc.—underneath all that is still the belief in guilt and punishment. You may think this or that person should be more perfect in your eyes, more pleasing in God's eyes. They should dress better, be neater, smarter, richer or whatever. Even if you say, "I have to perfect myself or be more perfect," that's a belief in guilt. Beneath all of that we're saying, "I'm better than they because at least I'm becoming a vegetarian.

I'm eating this and I'm not eating that," or "I'm better than the person who's eating meat"—all of which is still a belief in guilt.

Source is saying, "Who cares? I allow everything—fat, skinny, neat, dirty, hobo, mansion—I allow it all." Source cares more about the state of your inner world, which is what you will be looking at in your life review.

We are all immaculate conceptions. There's really no way out of Love, thank goodness! You will always be given further opportunities to choose and realize Love. Love will always be there for you whenever you are ready to accept it."

Q. *Are there examples of moments of pure Love?*

A. There are times when you bless or express Love with no agenda, or when you love another, desiring only their joy or happiness. These are moments of pure Love. Also include acts of courage for yourself or others, or acts of service to others done out of pure Love without expectation of being paid or getting a return. Love always returns in some way. Giving is receiving. Experiencing pure joy and delight are moments of pure Love.

Q. *When I see a lovely sunset, is that a moment of pure Love?*

A. Yes, it can be, when you are in communion with the sunset—when you recognize that the sunset is you and that you are the sunset—otherwise, it's just an experience of beauty. If the feeling of ecstasy you get from watching a beautiful sunset makes you feel loving or makes you feel a magnificence, it's an experience of Love.

An example of the pure Love is when you give as a natural extension of Love. When you give for the joy of giving, it is an act of sharing or joining. It comes from a natural desire to extend a hand out of kindness. More than that, it is a way of being, where you are Love itself—allowing, harmless in thought, word and action, desiring only to extend yourself as Love.

Consider these examples of Love in action: I was driving to Philadelphia to attend a seminar a few years ago and I had to cross a bridge. When I got to the other end of the bridge, there was a stoplight, and these young boys wanted to wash my windshield for money. I didn't want them to because I didn't have any extra money to give them. I had five dollars with me for lunch and that was it. I kept saying "No" to the boys. They ignored me and kept washing my windshield. I was watching how furious I was getting and thought, *Now I have to pay them* or *don't pay them, because they didn't listen to me.* Suddenly I heard Jesus's voice say to me, "That's *your* son." I felt Jesus meant it literally that these boys were as my own sons, my own children. I was so overcome by the truth of what I heard that I took out my fiver and I opened up the window and gave it to them.

When I got home that evening, my own three children had been busy making popsicle stick trivets during the day and they ran up to me saying, "Mommy, Mommy! We each sold a trivet today and we made $5.00!" It was so obvious that my willingness to give those boys my last $5.00 benefited my own children, proving that we are all in relationship with each other, a relationship that affects us all in each moment. I didn't want to give. I was in full judgment. When I got to the point where I was willing to give up my lunch money, it benefited my own children the very same day for the same amount of money.

Another time I had gotten in an argument with my former husband. I was really angry with him and I went down to the park. I was calling him every name in the book under my breath. I went and sat on a swing, fuming. Again, I heard Jesus's voice say to me, "You are making this up."

"What do you mean I'm making this up?" I asked.

"You *want* him to be guilty. You know, you could choose peace instead of this."

In that moment I realized *I didn't want to choose peace.* I had my reasons for being angry and I was sure that I was right. I also knew that what I was hearing from Jesus was correct. I sat with the whole thing for a long while and then I said out loud,

"Ok, I choose peace!"

At that moment the entire memory of the argument with my husband was erased from my mind. I literally couldn't remember what he and I had been arguing about. I tried to remember, *What was I mad about?* but I couldn't remember. Choosing peace literally erased the argument from my mind. When I got home, my husband wanted to chat about the argument and I said, "There's nothing to talk about because I can't remember any of it."

I had to have the willingness to see peace instead of guilt. When Jesus presented me with that choice, I got to see how much I *didn't* want to choose peace. It was an interesting exercise in the amount of judgment that goes on underneath the surface of our conscious awareness. Most often we aren't aware of the choices that could be made in any given situation. We certainly aren't aware in angry situations that we are making up the idea of someone opposing us in order to reinforce our belief in guilt. Actually, all situations devoid of peace are really asking for peace and that is our choice in those moments. Do we choose peace over anger or not? Seeing what we are willing or not willing to do shows us where we really are in our own consciousness.

Q. *You've been speaking about qualities of Love that seem to be big, universal qualities. Is the personal sense of love between two people a degree of universal Love?*

A. Two people in a relationship have opportunities to share love and become Love in the higher sense, but it's not a given that the attraction between two people is Love. The relationship is an opportunity to love and to practice Love.

You could have someone in your life to whom you are attracted, but then after a time the relationship may not stay loving, because the attraction lessens. You might still be attracted to the other person, but there may not always be loving behavior between you. Sometimes what is considered personal love turns into an exercise in making the other person feel guilty, which is obviously not an act of real Love. Nor are relationships based on physical attractions necessarily Love, although they could be.

Your own intimate relationships are exceptional opportunities because they're in your reality every day and you can see yourself mirrored in another. You can take what you learn and extend that way of being to those whom you meet. Each relationship is an opportunity to practice and learn about Love. We're always practicing either Love or judgment.

You can do the ascension process with another person if you both truly practice and actualize Love. On the other hand, you could choose to be single and do it with the whole world. You do not have to live with someone with whom you're incompatible or where there's neglect or abuse going on. Loving another person in higher Love does not mean you accept bad behavior from anyone!

In a compatible relationship, both people are *consciously* practicing and actualizing Love. In relationships where mistreatment, control or abuse is present, real Love is **not** present, so no real relationship is happening. In these cases, the loving thing to do is to realize that both people would be better off letting go of an unloving situation where the willingness to become Love is not present.

Love upholds the highest standards. It is an act of higher Love to make choices that uphold yourself in loving ways. Do not accept abuse or mediocrity for yourself or for those you love. Hold all to the highest victory in your heart and walk away from situations or people that do not reflect that.

Q. *When couple feel love, why do breakups happen?*

A. Breakups happen because one or the other, or both, aren't willing to love or they may be meant to go in different directions for further growth or to fulfill a particular path. It can also be about learning that attractions aren't always Love, which I mentioned earlier. When two people say they love one another, they demonstrate it by seeing each other in their innocence.

Q. I'm trying to get past the Catholic idea of "til death do us part". If one is not practicing forgiveness and the other is, can it be a more loving thing to separate, even if it violates the laws of religious belief?

A. It can be the more loving thing to separate because you're not in a real relationship if it's based on making the other guilty. Ultimately, it doesn't matter if you stay together or break up. There's no judgment around it. The decision has more to do with whether or not you are practicing Love together. Love has the power to transform any negativity where there is a willingness, but sometimes the loving act is to release one another from the relationship.

Q. So, we are Love ourselves?

A. That's right. You have a choice to resonate with it and keep merging with it in an ever-expanding way or deny it, in which case you will feel separate and alone by your own decision.

Remember that Love *is*. There is nothing we can do to change what Source created. Love is always there whenever we are ready to live out of that reality and that's why whatever you do or don't do doesn't change the fact that Love *is*. The quality of your own experience of Love is directly proportional to your willingness to choose it.

Q. *Will we recognize this change?*

A. Yes and you will feel it. People are already feeling it, actually. I get calls from people saying they know that they are changing; it's happening in varying degrees with people from all walks of life. They are becoming more aware of Love, telepathy and past-life memories. They are desiring different foods and are seeing and feeling more unity. Love always is accompanied by feelings of peace and a knowing that all is well.

Q. *How can I determine whether my self-love is selfish?*

A. Being loving to yourself is a natural result of finding out that we are all innocent and composed of Love. When we truly understand that we're not guilty, it's easy to be loving. There's nothing wrong with self-love; in fact, it is one of the most important things that is required for complete Love. If you don't love yourself enough to be good to yourself, you will not be able to be good to others. Choose higher standards for yourself—this will bring Love into your reality. Remember, it's about the quality of our choices—the higher the quality, the more refined the Love.

Let's talk about the judgment that people place on the path of service vs. the path of self-love. The path of Love is one, all-inclusive path. You can't truly give to others if you don't love yourself—you will see it as sacrifice. How will you know that everyone deserves the highest degree of Love if you can't allow yourself to have it? We're talking about giving up the belief in guilt for all time, for everyone, regardless of who they are and what they've done—including ourselves. When we can truly do that, loving ourselves will be easy and sensible. If there's a decision that you need to make that is self-nurturing, you'll know to make it, which may mean saying "No" to certain people, circumstances or ways of life. On the other hand, if there's someone to whom you need to give, you'll know that too and you'll naturally respond to them.

Making the choice for yourself to say "No" to certain things or people who make you feel worse about yourself is a victory for everyone. Choose to believe that we are all good and deserve only good. It's all or nothing.

Q. *Will I ever find true love or is it my feeling of guilt that's bringing all this unhappiness upon me?*

A. Check to see if you have released your judgment of others and yourself in order to find and remember true Love. If you were truly to do that, who knows how that would play out in your everyday life?

You could suddenly encounter Love in places you didn't before. Others around you may suddenly seem different. Or, your whole relationship could blow up and fall apart, leaving an opening for someone more loving to come in. You could move to Spain by yourself and be blissfully happy.

You really don't know the form it will take, but the reason you can't experience it yet could be because you still may not believe you can have it. That's when you ask for help. Ask a higher part of yourself to help you. Say,

"I'm willing to see things differently."

Participant: "I have been doing that and things have changed around in the last few days. I'm more peaceful now."

Aingeal: "It will keep increasing. The more you do it, the more you'll apply it to everyone and everything. Like attracts like."

Q. *My problem with Christianity has to do with Love. In Islam it's Allah is merciful. Is mercy different than Love?*

A. Christians may say they're about Love, but Muslim and Christians alike still project judgment and guilt onto each other. Each religion's version of mercy isn't that everyone is guiltless—it's that people are guilty, and now they're going to receive mercy.

Christianity believes in sin and then you're forgiven the sin. Both religions are judgment based. If you look closely, you'll find there's usually judgment first and then there's forgiveness. If it's Christian, it is forgiveness; if it's Islam, it is mercy. If these religions were truly based in Love, they wouldn't see each other as enemies or as separate. "My God's right. Your God is wrong"—that nonsense wouldn't exist. We still assassinate or threaten those who try to bring peace.

Choosing *only* Love is a decision—a choice—all or nothing. You're either choosing to see and be only Love or you're not. So, if someone is saying, "I'm going to be merciful, you thief! I'm going to only cut off your right ear instead of both ears"—that's hardly loving. You can't say that being kind and only half-killing the criminal is merciful or loving.

Merciful to most people is, "I could punish you, but I won't. I'll overlook it. I'll forgive it. I'll only punish you a little." It's still the judgment game. It's still making somebody guilty first.

Merciful forms of forgiveness can actually be dangerous when we make someone guilty first and then say we're going to forgive them. We only reinforce the belief in guilt.

The greatest gift we give anyone is to know they're innocent. We give up our belief in judgment, even if the other person doesn't. They may still think they're guilty or horrible or think they've made too many mistakes and they're worthless. You can't change that for them because that's their decision, but you can see them innocent and by doing so, you're donating grace to them. That grace may be what tips the scales for them one day.

My Dad in the last few years of his life started being verbally abusive to my Mother. He had a bit of a temper at times, but this was worse. He had an unusual cold that didn't go away for months. A year later, he came down with throat cancer and he asked my sister, "Do you think this is God punishing me for what I said to your Mother?" My sister told him "Yes" because she was mad at my Father, which of course reinforced his guilt. But the truth is that the answer was "No." It's not God punishing him—it was my Father punishing himself.

We are not saying that people don't do things that are unloving or criminal; we are saying that the repair is to affirm that they deserve Love, no matter what. You can put a criminal in jail so they don't project their own guilt onto another person through violent actions. You can walk away from an abusive person and still know that they deserve to realize Love.

Walking away is you loving yourself and in so doing, you affirm Love. You make that affirmation not only for yourself, but also for anyone who may need the strength to make the same choice. We either bring the actuality of Love's presence into realization or we keep it hidden through our belief in guilt. Whatever we choose, Love still allows and is still present beneath everything.

Chapter Nine

Miracles

Miracles

Aingeal: "As I said the opening prayer, the room filled with red light—the same light that appeared during the sessions on *Trees* and *The Art of Prosperity*."

Q. *Why is red light connected to Miracles, Prosperity and Trees?*

A. The red light is from the violet light spectrum. The violet light spectrum is inherent in all life in this dimension, even though it operates in a higher frequency range. It is the color of transmutation and forgiveness, which go hand in hand. Miracles come under the heading of the transmutation of matter or conditions. Prosperity works this way as well, as it is about turning poverty consciousness into prosperity consciousness or turning base thoughts into higher thoughts.

Red light has a lower frequency than violet light and is necessary to ground a Miracle or a transmutation into this physical plane, thus creating a different appearance. Using the principle of "As above, so below," we see violet being above and red being below.

Q. *What is a 'Miracle' and under what laws does it operate?*

A. A 'Miracle' alters the laws of physics in any given dimension. It intersects a paradigm vertically, allowing for a dimensional shift in the moment from one form or experience of reality to another. It replaces fear with Love. It corrects at the cellular level, but it also corrects the mind. It replaces disorder with Divine Order.

It comes from the Law of One, which recognizes God as One, Love as Law and Love as Order. Miracles correct perception and matter through the opening created by re-establishing Love. Miracles occur instantaneously because they do not follow, nor are they limited by the perceptions of time and space.

Q. *How can I say to a mountain, "Move" and it would move?*

A. It is possible because matter only *appears* solid. Everything is consciousness and density is only an agreement made by minds who are experimenting with the idea of separation. Remove the perception and belief in solidity and anything can move.

Q. *Is there such a thing as a bad miracle, or a miracle in reverse? If I create a bad effect, is that also a miracle?*

A. The Miracle I see is a change for the better based on Love, going from an unhealthy state to a healthy state; a change from a lower frequency to a higher frequency. More than that, it is re-establishing Source's intention for Life in a situation or condition that has forgotten it. This can occur on any level—spiritual, emotional, mental or physical. So, there are no bad Miracles.

Q. *When someone uses the forces of Nature to manifest something negative, is that a Miracle?*

A. This is the same question as the above. Do you think Source will give you a different answer? Miracles are from the Order of Love. Our ability to manifest desires in our lives using thought, intention and desire is indeed a miraculous *process* and implies we are all 'genie's'. We consciously use the Law of Cause and Effect when we do this. It's in the nature of the Life Principle. A Miracle is a phenomenon that instantly changes a physiology, a state of consciousness or an event without requiring the conscious intention of the receiver of the Miracle.

This makes it something of a different Order that operates under different Laws—specifically the Laws of Love, which automatically forgives all that Love is *not*. It follows that any state of consciousness that is not Love is unnatural.

Q. *Is the process of Miracles equivalent to the quantum field of subatomic particles where you hold the image of what it is that you desire to manifest and the image arranges the subatomic particles into your image?*

A. Again, this is the same question as the above. Miracles occur under the Laws of Love, which would be the Laws of communion and sharing. In your example, the Law of Cause and Effect is still in use and very often it only involves the separatist desires of the thinker. It is working on the level of mind, imagination and intention. Your intentions work quickly because beliefs alters the quantum field. Being a fluid field, it responds to your will and desire. A Miracle however, occurs without your conscious will and intention.

Q. *What happens to the body when it receives a Miracle?*

A. There is an immediate 'whitening' or 'purifying' effect in the body. You could say that all misperception is corrected. Time is suspended or interrupted in the moment and an alteration of the person's reality takes place, allowing for a dimensional shift to occur within the individual. This alters the individual's bodily programming, thus making the body 'new'.

Q. *Is a Miracle belief dependent for the receiver?*

A. No, a Miracle does not need belief to occur.

Q. *Can we say the creation of the human body is a Miracle? Whose intention was it?*

* * *

A. The Miracle of the body is the fact that the process of Creation itself is Divine—there's a divine blueprint for life that other beings may learn about and modify in various ways to create life forms. It doesn't mean that those who created various life forms or are doing cloning are highly spiritual or evolved beings because they're not *causing* Miracles; they're taking information from an existing design as a template to create new life forms. The Miracle in these cases is Life itself—the fact that Life *is*, that Life exists.

Q. *Is there a link between a Miracle and intuition?*

A. No, there is no link in the context in which we are speaking. Intuition belongs to your innate instinctual nature, while a Miracle is a spontaneous intervention in our paradigm from a different Order of reality. Knowing that something is going to happen before it happens for example, is not a Miracle. Intuition is something you were born with. It's part of the divine imprint of yourself. So, Source wouldn't call intuition a Miracle— It would say it's part of our inherent make-up, similar to how animals have instinct, plants know to face the Sun and close up at night, etc. You would say that these examples are evidence of the intelligence of Life built into every living thing.

Humans have their Instinctual Self as well, which we call our intuition, which allows us to receive impulses (illuminations) from Source that go beyond survival. We have the ability to discern many different frequency bands of information. The center of our intuition comes from our solar plexus area, which is why people say, "I have a gut feeling…"

However, there's a higher knowing that involves our entire system where every cell *knows* at the same moment. To use it we need to evolve to that level of knowing and awareness. This inner knowing is not a Miracle. A Miracle causes instantaneous change —a vertical intersection in our linear reality and does not require intuition. It alters the physical laws because it comes from a Field of Love that supersedes this reality and has no polarity or duality.

Q. *Are we also looking at personal power? In other words, if people were in their knowing, in their true spiritual connection to Source, could they perform Miracles?*

A. A person who has achieved this level will naturally radiate a vibration of Love that naturally allows Miracles to occur. There is no conscious need to 'perform' a Miracle.

Q. *I still hear quite a distinction between manifesting a desire and creating a Miracle. As our intentions become purer, will we be able to perform Miracles and manifest our desires more easily?*

A. Here's the distinction: You could have a black magician sitting here right now who knows that something will materialize because he's intending it to. That's just a fact. He could cause an instantaneous change, but that change wouldn't be a Miracle. A Miracle has Love and purity attached to it. A Miracle is an instantaneous expression of Love. The manifesting process—if it's devoid of love—is not considered a Miracle. When someone intends something dark or negative, their resulting manifestation will eventually compact in on itself.

When something compacts, ultimately it will turn in on itself and be destroyed. When this happens, it goes under the heading of death, or 'molecular compaction'. A Miracle, on the other hand, promotes more Life. It causes life expansion or *correction*, rather than contraction.

If someone has a desire to manifest something in their lives and the desire is not ill-intended, they may do so, knowing that the power of thought and desire are the key components of manifesting. This is fine to do, but it is still not a Miracle—it is 'manifesting'.

A Miracle is Love in action, devoid of the necessity for anyone to think about it or 'perform' it. It comes from the Field of Love, which is not affected by anything here.

Q. *If everything is perception, where do Miracles fit in?*

A. True communication with Source and with 'All That Is' automatically causes Miracles. It is a consequence of real Love, which is communion and acceptance of all life. Communion dissolves perception, which is an aspect of the belief in separateness. The Miracle comes from Source or Love, which is beyond perception. Love is a reality in which there is no duality. Love can intersect this or any other dimension at any point and alter its physics because it comes from a place where only Love, or Unity resides which is also Divine Order. There is neither perceived separation or division; nor is there guilt or judgment.

Q. *Are Miracles happening now? How many, like, 100 a day?*

A. Oh, much more than that! More than thousands are happening daily. We just don't hear about them. *(Suddenly the room is full of orbs!)*

Q. *Can orbs facilitate a Miracle? Are they connected?*

A. My feeling about the orbs in this room is that they came in to listen. They're very interested in what goes on in certain places. Source wouldn't say, "Go to the orbs for a Miracle." Source would say, "For a Miracle, go to Love, which is the Realm of Source."

Can orbs perform Miracles? "No!". Orbs are manifestations of thought. They come from the billions of thought forms that humanity thinks or imagines daily. Many orbs have become actual beings; others have coalesced into colors or geometric patterns. For this reason, orbs can be perceived as 'visitors' in that they are thought forms that have become conscious, or 'alive'.

When orbs appear in a room, they oftentimes are parts of consciousness traveling and stopping to listen. Once an orb has become conscious, it can learn and evolve in that consciousness.

Q. *I feel that there are Miracles happening every moment of every day and even here in this room. You can say it's a Miracle that I got here, that we drove along in the car and that we survived driving through traffic. Aren't these all Miracles? What one person sees as a big Miracle, someone else may see as a small Miracle.*

A. In those examples, yes, *Life* is a Miracle—the fact that Life is here and it all works, is definitely a Miracle. The Miracle that is Life is one level of Miracle. The other is when our physical Laws are reversed—such as an interruption in the Law of Cause and Effect, where the outcome of a situation is altered and pure Love enters in. In those cases, we are talking of a Higher Order that comes into effect that intersects our linear reality and causes either a reversal or a complete change in a condition, state of mind, event or situation instantaneously.

We are distinguishing this Miracle as an *event or occurrence* distinct from the Miracle we call Life.

Q. *You said that all Miracles have Love attached to them. That's a beautiful concept. but are there also degrees of Love? Let's say that a girl is ill and her Mother unconditionally loves her and desires that she be well. If she dies, is it because her Mother didn't love her enough?*

A. No. This child, depending on her own soul journey, is either going to heal or die depending on her soul contract. If someone wants to develop a particular quality or virtue before they leave this world, a Miracle may actually interfere with that purpose. We are all here doing many things, and each of us has had a hand in orchestrating our soul contracts before we entered this world.

Miracles and Love do allow our contracts to be suspended or altered for higher purposes, but such changes would be made by a Higher Law other than ourselves.

Q. *My husband and I went to Lourdes seven times for our three sons. We deeply believed and prayed that our children would be cured. Could our children's illnesses have been part of their soul journeys, which is why they weren't cured? We believed a Miracle would occur because it had supposedly happened for others there.*

A. Remember in another group session we asked about your deceased sons and we talked to them? We saw that it was in their soul contracts to leave when they did and also, that they had wanted to stay together. I know it's hard to accept that when they're your children, but it had a lot to do with them being together and not being apart.

Q. *My other son is ill and I know he doesn't want to live. He wants to be with my other sons who have crossed.*

A. The difference here is that there's a part of your son now that doesn't want to take the responsibility for living, which is why he is being asked if he wants to live. I wouldn't assume that his soul contract is the same as your other children. Your remaining son has had other lives in which he's given up on living, where he hasn't really pushed hard enough. He's a soul that's being tested with challenges in order for him to push through and succeed this time. I don't see that his soul contract is to die young. He's causing that to happen. He can get well if he makes the decision to do so and maybe you could facilitate that by talking to him. It is his liver that is sick and the word 'live' is in the word 'liver'. The liver filters the blood and the blood is the lifeforce energy, so if he's losing lifeforce energy, it suggests that he doesn't want to live. He will heal when he decides that he wants to live. He can turn this around for himself.

Q. *Is there any difference between a body receiving a Miracle and Alchemy, where someone turns a substance from one thing into another, or the performance of magic on some level?*

* * *

A. You're talking about two different things. Magic is different from Alchemy. When a base metal is turned into gold, it is working within the physical Laws of Nature. You could say in a way, that Miracles are Alchemy insofar as they transmute something from one form to another, but a Miracle is not coming *from* the physical laws of Nature—it is *altering* the physical laws in an instant. It is rearranging elements and forming them into something new. Turning base metals into gold is a long, lengthy process taking years, but it can be done.

Magic is different because it is the calling in of various forces, substances and spirits to effect a change. It doesn't necessarily use Love as an abiding principle. It incorporates rituals and other talismans to cause a desired effect or outcome. It would still come under the Law of Cause and Effect. Magic is very different than the Miracle we've been talking about, where it's an action or intention based on pure Love and knowing.

Q. *What is star energy and has it to do with Miracles?*

A. Nuclear fusion. Star energy can drastically change form from one state to another. Its blue-white fire core is literally inherent within everyone. However, it is not activated in most of us. If it were activated, Miracles would be occurring naturally. Scientifically, physically, we are formed from star elements.

You can realize your connection or communion with Source through meditating on your 'star seed' by focusing on the tip of your sternum just below your breasts. This area is a gateway to the remembrance of your origin and your connection and interrelationship with all life, which is Love. To connect with this part of yourself, sit or lay quietly and focus your attention inward on your sternum. Keep focusing there and intend to connect with your own star essence within. You may feel an opening there, or heat. You can ask this star point to heal your body of any affliction. Allow this energy to go to where you need it. Come out of the meditation when you feel ready. You can repeat this meditation whenever you like.

Chapter Ten

Dreams

Dreams

Aingeal: "With our questions about Dreams, we found that there are many levels to dreams and many dimensions intersecting other dimensions in the dream state. Therefore, some of the questions have multiple levels to the answer."

Q. *What are Dreams and what is their purpose?*

A. Dreams are composed of ribbons of color or color bands. They are part of a wave movement that is happening around and through us continually. They flow and congeal into various shapes and then move on. They appear transient, yet they are very alive and dynamic.

The purpose of Dreams is multifaceted—they bring in light (color nourishment) to rejuvenate us, and they bring understanding and enlightenment to us. They are a medium for our creative minds to manifest and express our desires and see our fears. They can be a bridge between worlds and dimensions. Dream frequencies interact with our brainwaves while we sleep. If we were aware of these living color frequencies during the day, we would be able to receive them and be nourished by them throughout the day without thought interference. We wouldn't have such a great need to sleep, because we would be revitalized constantly. While we are using our brain frequencies during the day to think, decide, observe and receive data, we are not conscious of dream frequencies. Sleeping is a time when these color frequencies can come in freely and communicate through myriads of expressions.

This level of dream energy is designed to bring more light into our bodies to replenish and nourish us. This revitalization process could take the form of a dream in which you are reviewing events that occurred during the day or some other situation in your life. These alive and conscious color bands help process events in your life to bring you back into balance. If you didn't have an issue or event that needed to be processed or balanced, these color bands would still be in your sleep process, bringing more light and color into your consciousness and body. Often dreams are about organization and putting something in your life back in order.

Q. *Is there a particular place in our physiology or our brains from which dreams originate?*

A. There doesn't seem to be a particular location in our physiology or our brain, but dreams do have to do with the way our brain fires or is firing when we sleep.

Q. *Do our brains and the nerve network in our solar plexus connect to our dreams?*

A. No, the nerve network in the solar plexus connects to the mass consciousness. It has a horizontal movement to it, and connects to things linear. Brain chemistry, in contrast, is nonlocal and its firings go off sporadically in many different directions. It's interrelating with the Field on various electrical levels, which is why the brain is the relay station between many different dimensional levels.

Q. *Within our time reality, how long does a dream last?*

A. The average dream is 30 seconds to a minute, but some can last up to five minutes. Most don't last longer than that. You're in 'no-time' when you dream—time collapses in the dream state.

Q. Do we continually get depleted of colors and light?

A. Yes, we are made of color, light and sound. We do get depleted of these elements in our daily lives. Colors have a very strong connection to the minerals in our bodies. During times of stress, we become depleted in various colors, sounds and minerals. Minerals are very important to us because it is through them that we absorb color and sound frequencies into our bodies. Therefore, if your body is deficient in minerals, you will not be able to absorb the amount of color frequencies you need to keep yourself enlivened and in balance, even if you were out in the sunlight all day. Dreaming rebalances and replenishes us.

Q. What does it mean if you dream in black and white?

A. When this happens, you have ventured into an alternate reality that can be called a 'hibernation zone'. These zones are not necessarily positive. This is how you can tell that you're in a negative place. These are alternate dimensions that are devoid of of light and color. Finding yourself in one of these places while sleeping can help you understand how to deal with negativity. This can be a signal that you may be deficient in certain vitamins and minerals, or that you may be becoming ill and need to check in on yourself.

Q. When did dreaming become necessary?

A. We have had the ability to dream since we have been in dense physical bodies and began to lose our memory of who we are. We have dreamt since we lost the ability to communicate with all life everywhere. Dreaming isn't only a human quality—animals also dream. The ability to dream is within any species that has a brain. It is how species get nourished and process the events of their lives.

Q. *Is anything possible in dreams?*

A. Dream states are not subject to the same laws of gravity that are present in our conscious state. The color frequency bands in dreams are free flowing and do not have the density to them that we have while we are in our bodies. Thought is continually creative, but it may take longer for our thoughts to manifest in our physical reality than in a dream precisely because our 3D reality is denser and the color frequencies or elements needed to easily manifest may not be present. In the dream state, we do not have this densification or color deficiency that we experience in our physical reality. Therefore, our thoughts can manifest instantaneously in the dream state.

Q. *Is there any way we can be more active or conscious in the dream state and use our dreams more productively?*

A. Our Spirits would love us to be more consciously aware while in the dream state. There are many books on 'Lucid Dreaming' that teach how to be 'awake' while in the dream state so that you can influence the progression and outcome of dreams. If you put more attention on this and make it an actual discipline, you would see physical reality differently and manifest your desires more rapidly. Your dream state and your conscious waking state become one continuous flow.

When we go into a dream state, it feels like an entirely different reality from our waking state. However, when we become *conscious* dreamers, we can control the outcome of dreams by making choices *while in the dream*. This helps us in our waking lives with direction and clarity of purpose. In other words, our lives become more deliberate and focused with much greater meaning and purpose. We could wake up remembering a discussion we had with our Guides. There would be no separation between waking and sleeping. Discipline is required however, and it requires practice.

* * *

Q. *Where do we go when we dream?*

A. Actually, we don't *go* anywhere; we interact with levels that are already around us. I'm being shown a large circular sphere of energy. We interact with this sphere constantly not only when we sleep, but also when we're awake. We just aren't conscious that we are doing so.

Q. *Since dreaming is an interaction with the surrounding dimensional levels, are we accessing something new or do dreams form from what occurs in our awake state?*

A. Both. However, dreaming wouldn't be necessary if we were in a more conscious alignment with this field around us that is interacting with us all the time. Dreaming occurs because we are not consciously aware.

Think of it like frequencies accessible on a radio station. If we were more conscious of this field around us and of the living colors that interact with us, their integration into our lives would occur throughout the day rather than just while we sleep.

Dreaming occurs because we become depleted and need to be revitalized by these color rays. Since our consciousness is only focused in a linear fashion, we are not aware of the communication that goes on between the many different levels surrounding us. Therefore, we inadvertently block the integration or flow of various nourishing lifeforce energies.

Can you imagine what a greater effect these color waves could have on us if we each were in a conscious co-creative relationship with them throughout the day? When we direct our attention to so many other things that really have little importance, we block our own awareness of these other levels of reality. Therefore, we are not aware of the communication that we have with all life and because we are not aware of this communication, our ability to consciously interact with it is diminished. Think of your consciousness as nerves or wires that need to be kept free-flowing in order to have a give-and-take type of reception.

When we use our thoughts to focus on things that cause static in this communication system, we can't receive the messages from the relationships between us, others and the Universe. Because of these disruptions, sleep is necessary to temporarily close off our conscious mind so we can replenish without interference. Dreaming is a consequence of our linear focus of attention.

Nourishing energy, our Spirit Guides and other levels of our subconscious all need to have a way to get through to us because our minds are never quiet during the day. Jiddu Krisnamurti once said that if we were consciously awake, we would have no need to dream. He encouraged us to begin a conscious relationship with our dream state and with everyday reality.

Q. *Does it follow then that those who don't dream or remember their dreams are healthier than those who do?*

A. No, we can't deduce that. People still dream, even if they don't remember their dreams. When someone has reached the state where they no longer need to dream, they will be fully conscious and will know they are. Most people are unconscious and still dream because they need to be replenished or nourished. Some people are awake at these levels and don't need to dream, but they are exceptions rather than the rule.

Q. *Who are the people in our dreams?*

A. They can be symbolic representations of aspects of ourselves taking on particular forms to get a message across to us or they can be a visit from someone in another plane of existence. Many of the 'actors' we see in dreams are aspects of ourselves, so we can become aware of these aspects. They appear in certain ways, doing certain things because of the associations we make in our minds about our world and our lives. At other times, these actors can be fragments of our own consciousness from our own thoughts, beliefs and desires.

If we are not consciously aware of the symbolism in our lives, things will be arranged for us in the dream state to help us become aware of certain things. Many things happen in the dream state—guidance is received; our color frequencies are adjusted for nourishment purposes; we process out events in our everyday life and we may be actively traveling to other dimensions or carrying out missions.

Those who show up in our dreams portray themselves in certain roles and sequences, have everything to do with whatever we may need to see or have affirmed. Perhaps we are being warned of something that could show up in our everyday reality—something we need to look at or change. We'll know because of the emotional impact the dream has on us when we awaken.

I've had dreams affect me emotionally that I thought meant a certain thing but when I journaled about what the dream meant to me, its message was different than what I originally thought.

Something that can feel ominous in a dream can actually be a very high message about transformation in our life. It's a good idea to look at dreams as symbolic dramas that show us something about ourselves and what we're doing or not doing in our lives. Start by asking yourself what the scenes and sequences in a dream *mean* to you, because everything in our consciousness is associative or has a symbolic meaning to us on a subconscious level and it is all very personal to each of us.

You may meet alternate selves in the dream state. These are versions of you living in different dimensional spaces having their own lives. It doesn't matter whether these alternate selves are fragments of your thoughts and desires playing themselves out or actual aspects of your soul. If they show up in your dream, look into what they mean to you and you will make progress in understanding the workings of your own being, whether on the 3D or multidimensional levels.

Remember, we are in relationship with our other selves even if we are not consciously aware of them and what they do in their dimensions affects us here and vice-versa.

***

There is an active relationship going on continually between what happens with our thoughts and our brain chemistry and how that gets translated to the different dimensional levels around us. A co-creative process is happening between our thoughts, feelings and beliefs and the forms, colors, and shapes they become in this reality and other realities. The dream state doesn't act *upon* you; rather it is *responding to* your quality and what your consciousness is emitting.

The alternate dimension you experience may be guided or directed by a higher aspect of you, depending on what message you may need to decipher from the formations that your own consciousness is displaying. This is the opportunity that our internal guidance uses to give us a message or direction when we wouldn't be aware of it in our waking consciousness.

Not all dreams are important messages—some may just be the healing or the de-stressing of events that have occurred through the day. However, it is important to look at what aspects of your daily life are appearing in your dream state, because there could be some important information there for you to examine.

If we were more conscious in our everyday life of the different dimensional levels around us, we would be co-creating much more often with much greater clarity and focus. If we were more conscious, we wouldn't need to receive guidance in our dream state. Instead, we would be consciously and consistently interacting with our own guidance throughout the day. We would also be fed throughout the day by color and light, because we wouldn't be using our brain power for decisions or actions that deplete our energy. Instead, we would be in the flow of life, which would be one continuous action without the need to sleep and dream to replenish ourselves. We would be more in the Moment.

Dreams about certain people can be a message or warning for or from them, or they can represent some aspect of them, you, or both that needs your attention. The fact that they show up in your dream means that you can offer them healing or a blessing, which may make a difference in both your lives.

Do not assume that dreaming about death or illness concerning someone you know means that such a condition is coming to that person. Sometimes it is a person's Spirit asking you to convey a message about something he/she may need to take care of. Always offer a blessing or healing energy in these cases.

Q. *Do the thought forms or beings that appear in dreams come down into this physical reality?*

A. Particular beings or events can materialize into this physical reality from the dream state, because we are co-creating with ourselves through the process of dreaming. This is also why it is a good idea to become a conscious dreamer so that we are deliberately choosing what we would like to bring back from alternate dimensions to enhance our present physical reality. Usually actors or events in a dream do not materialize for any lasting period of time because the dreamer does not focus on them long enough for them to become solidified or lasting in this dimension. We need to know though, that any thought form we create can attach itself to other people with similar energy and become something more, even if we ourselves are not energizing it; this is true, whether we are waking or dreaming.

Here is a story in which my dream state and my everyday reality merged. I was asleep and dreaming that I was walking through a forest. I was aware of a dark cloud above the tree line that was following me throughout the dream. It felt very evil and ominous. I was trying to get away from it and trying to find my way out of the forest. I could see a clearing and a light at the edge of the forest, but every time I took a step in that direction, the dark cloud would advance upon me. It seemed there was no way out of this. Just at that moment, my dog in my everyday life began to bark, waking me up from my dream. My husband got up to check the house to see if there was someone in the house. When he went to turn on the lights, he found the power was out.

This was very strange, as there were no storms in the area to cause such a power outage. While my husband was checking the house, I lay in my bed thinking that I couldn't leave the dream that way. I had to go back into the dream and try to overcome the evil presence. My husband came back and said there was nothing strange going on in the house and we went back to sleep. I immediately fell back into the dream and it continued exactly where it had left off before I awoke. I was still fearful of not being able to find a way out of the forest and in my mind I called the police. The police arrived immediately and looked up at the dark cloud looming above us and told me this was out of their league. They said they couldn't help me.

Suddenly a voice said, "There is only one God." As soon as I heard it, the dark cloud disappeared and I was at the edge of the forest and out into the sunshine. At that moment, the power came back on, the alarm went off and all the lights came on in the house. What happened? There really had been an evil energy present during the night. The dream was letting me know what was going on. How it ended up had a lot to do with the voice that came in to remind me there was only one God—in essence One True Reality in which evil does not exist. As soon as that reality intersected that of the negative forces, the negative forces disappeared. The point is, evil is based on false perceptions of reality and is not a living presence in and of itself.

This is a case where Higher Guidance was at work teaching me a valuable lesson. In the dream, I was being threatened by dark forces and in extreme fear. However, another part of me intersected the reality where only Truth exists. When this happens, you are in a reality based on safety, love and support. This evidenced itself in my physical waking state by the power coming back on at the same moment. The dark cloud could have been a malevolent ET abduction attempt which my higher Guides thwarted by waking me up with my dog barking, and second, by getting a Truth message to me when I went back into the dream the second time.

Since ET ships often affect the power in the areas they appear, it would make sense that the power would go off and then back on again when the dark cloud left. Perhaps the dark cloud was actually a cloaked ship.

Q. *Do our dreams form out of our own experiences or do we actively create the dream scenario as we go along?*

A. There can be times during the night when you are processing your waking 3D life and another part of the night where your Guides are downloading scenes or information to help you. While you're sleeping, you can sometimes float off into an entirely different dimension where you've never been before. It may be positive or negative.

Sometimes dreams are your subconscious giving you a measure of progress in your life or as a soul. For example, it may show you what your attitude is or it may play out a scenario to let you know what you've been doing with yourself—what your thoughts have been manifesting for good or ill. It's important to look at all dreams as symbolic dramas giving you a message about yourself on various levels.

If you get proficient at paying attention to your dreams, you will notice that each dream carries a particular energy or feeling with it that will help you determine what type of dream it is. A given dream might help with your everyday experiences, like rejuvenating yourself or relieving stress; it might be a message from your Higher Guidance. A frightful dream may be evidence that you wandered into a dimension that isn't so positive, while a happy dream may suggest that you have visited somewhere that is euphoric.

In my story above, the dream had many layers. It was an actual event that was happening on a dream level, but it was also happening in my everyday life as it had turned the power off in my house. I was under some type of threat and my Higher Guidance came into the dream to help me—most likely because I was asking for help (calling the police in my dream).

I was also learning a lesson about the Truth of only one God and of how any other reality different from that is not real. It was also a test of my courage by me going back into the dream to overcome the fear and the evil presence.

Some types of dreams can be prophetic—as in doomsday scenarios or some other type of disaster. In these cases, the dream can be an implant by negative beings. What I mean by this is that sometimes negative entities use a person's dream state to create images of doomsday scenarios as a way of using the dreamer's mind and emotional body to encourage disastrous events in the 3D world. Many people who experience prophetic dreams and then see that they have manifested in 3D think this is proof that they are tuned in to the future or are highly intuitive. However, what can really be going on is that they are being used by dark forces to create catastrophic scenarios on Earth. Anyone having a doomsday dream should quickly reverse the scenario with their thoughts by asserting that all is well and no disaster will occur. In this way, they contribute to a positive future instead of energizing a doomsday future. Dark forces know the power of imagery and how our emotional bodies can create futures based on pictures and feelings, which is why they use *us* to create doomsday events in our world.

One recurring dream I have exemplifies Higher Guidance. I dream that I am about to board a huge white jumbo jet. I need to get to the gate on time and I find interferences or obstacles in my way. Sometimes I get on board just in time by some fluke, while at other times I don't make the flight. Sometimes the jet is already in flight and I am on my way to somewhere very beautiful, loving and bright. Usually I know the people on board the jet are soul friends whom I've known for many years and my husband is always traveling with me. Other times, I will be getting off the jumbo jet at some new place and find there are ETs in this new place, all of whom I know. The symbolism of the white jumbo jet always lets me know that this is an important dream—a measure of my spiritual progress or lack of progress, depending on how it turns out.

If we were conscious dreamers, we would make choices in our dreams so they would turn out great which would affect our everyday lives by putting us on tracks that support our highest growth and progress. By becoming conscious dreamers, we will gain greater degrees of control over the outcomes of our dreams and we will be able to interact with their various levels consciously. As conscious dreamers, we change the scenarios of many aspects of our dreams in varying dimensions by consciously choosing our outcomes. We no longer have to feel that we are victims of forces outside ourselves in our dreams. This practice will also help us merge different levels of reality into our 3D waking life so that they serve our highest desires, rather than thwart us in our progress.

Q. *So, the more conscious we become in our dreams, the stronger our consciousness will become in our waking life. Is that right?*

A. Yes, that's right. The stronger you are in your own consciousness, the less you are affected by negative forces. You begin to see there is no separation between your subconscious and your conscious mind—nothing need be unconscious to you any longer. The greater your degree of conscious awareness, the more deeply you will know yourself. You will also begin to see the symbolism and connections in your 3D waking life in the events and situations in which you find yourself.

You will understand the thoughts and beliefs beneath any experience or situation. You will also understand what is being reflected back to you. You will be able to consciously make decisions in your 3D life much more easily because you will have clarity on what the choices are and what they mean.

The idea there is a barrier between the conscious mind and the subconscious mind is an error. It is only because we do not understand the language of symbolism and reflection in our lives that it appears that we are unaware of things that are going on beneath the surface of our conscious mind.

The fun part of becoming a conscious dreamer is when you see the intentions you have manifested in your dreamstate appear in your 3D reality.

When people die or have a near-death experience (NDE), they usually find themselves in a place of knowledge and understanding. Suddenly, they see how everything is related and how everything makes sense. All the pieces fit into place. Things of which they were unaware in their 3D lives suddenly all flow together and they get to see life as a single movement of consciousness. It isn't necessary to die or to have an NDE for this awareness. It can be done by becoming a conscious dreamer or by learning to see the symbolism in your everyday life.

Q. *Can a conscious dreamer heal others from the dream state?*

A. Yes, with their permission. It can be more powerful to consciously manifest from the dream state.

Q. *If you do something like that without permission, would you invite the same kind of intrusion upon yourself?*

A. You could and you would also be creating karmic chords with the person you're trying to heal, which means that you have taken on some of their karmic burden by becoming involved in their energy without their permission. It's actually a loving thing *not to* interfere in another person's situation unless you are asked. Some situations people are in are because they are being challenged to become more masterful in some way.

Q. *Can anybody or anything monitor our dreams?*

A. Other aspects of you can watch your dreams. You interact with higher parts of yourself all day long, especially in your dream state, because the barriers to 3D waking consciousness are not there. If something is playing out in a dream that is the result of your own thought processes, I don't see the other aspects of yourself interfering with the process, but they may watch it unfold. It might manifest as a message that helps you in your 3D life. If you allow them to inspire you, they will send you frequencies when they find an opening.

Let's say a higher part of me wanted to interact with the 3D me during the day. It could be difficult for it to get through because I'm busy and my mind is filled with thoughts of what I'm doing. In this case, the higher parts of me would probably continue doing their own thing on their own levels until I am sleeping, when I may be more available for communication.

Q. *If I want to see life more clearly, can I ask for clarity?*

A. Yes, of course. It's a good idea to practice this, so you establish a conscious rapport between your conscious self and your dream state self. You've probably heard that it's good to record your intentions in a notebook before you go to sleep.

Then, when you wake up, no matter what time it is, immediately write out your dream in your notebook before you forget it. Once sunlight emerges, cascades of waking hormones are released and the process of forgetting ensues.

Q. *When someone wishes you "sweet dreams" before you go to bed at night, what kind of effect does it have on your dreams?*

A. It's a nice sentiment to offer someone when they go to sleep at night, but the truth is that a person's own consciousness follows its own journey when it is sleeping. What the sentiment will do is offer someone a greater degree of comfort in a dream. Ultimately, it is the person's own consciousness and what's going on with them that determines the quality of their dream state.

Q. *What is good to say to children before they sleep?*

A. Don't forget that children as well as adults are still under the protection of their Holy Guardian Angel and it might be a good idea to call on that Presence to be active with them throughout their sleeping/dream state. We need to remember that Angels are evolving too. They may not always be available or 'on duty' to serve you. The same is true of the Holy Guardian Angel. Your Holy Guardian Angel will know if you are in danger, but it may not always interact in every aspect of your life. It may be on another project or doing something in another dimension, for example. If you deliberately call on your Holy Guardian Angel before going to sleep and ask it to provide a particular service, it will guarantee to be there.

Q. *Can one's dreams be infiltrated by negative forces?*

A. If there is negative energy in the vicinity of your dreaming and you are vulnerable, it's possible that negative energy could interfere with your thought processes.

Keep in mind however, that on some level, there is always a resonance between the negative energies' frequency and your own. Remember, 'like attracts like'. Earth is always turning and at times parts of it align with certain grid patterns, and at other times it aligns with other grid patterns. It's the same for us when we sleep. The particular time when you go out of your body to sleep is subject to the grid patterns in place.

The configurations of the grids of the planet determine the kind of energy or place you initially slip into. If you feel vulnerable or upset when you go to sleep and there is a likeness in the ethers at that moment, you could easily slip into a different dimensional space that vibrates at a lower frequency. You may find yourself amongst beings that are also vibrating at a low frequency, which is why the practice of Lucid Dreaming is useful. You will realize you are dreaming and be able to choose yourself out of a particular dream or space that you find unpleasant.

Q. *Are we more powerful in dreamstate than when awake?*

A. Not necessarily. It isn't that the dreamstate is more powerful than the waking state. You are always powerful. It's just that your logical mind isn't interrupting you in the dreamstate with useless thoughts and perceptions.

Q. *Are dreams more real than 3D reality?*

A. No. This idea comes from the thought that there is some division or separation between worlds in which one world may seem more real than another. Shamans call the subconscious world 'The Dreamtime', implying it was a place of archetypal images that was somehow more real than our waking world. It only *appears* to be separate because we have not yet developed our consciousness to the point where we can be awake to the various levels of our own being or to the collective unconscious.

Q. *Is our 3D level of reality also a dream?*

A. On a certain level, it's all a dream. You could say that Creation and all image making is a dreamscape in the sense that we are imagining it all, or coming to conclusions about reality and then seeing it manifest before our eyes. We're making it all up as we go along, but there is a core Truth in Creation—and that is the Love that is behind all powers of manifestation.

It is obvious we don't always create loving manifestations. The principle that allows image making to congeal into a manifestation is still the Life Principle behind the scenes. In this way, you can see that you either make your own heaven or your own hell; you feel as limited or unlimited as you believe. When you know this, the possibilities are endless as to what you can experience according to your beliefs.

Ultimately, if you play with manifestation, you will eventually want to experience only pure Love. You will recognize that all other scenarios are ideas of consciousness playing themselves out according to your desires. When you get to the place where you desire to be only Love, your creations will be entirely different.

Q. Does everyone dream the same way?

A. Everyone has the same *potential* in their dreaming states, but not everyone has the same language in their dreams. Since the language of dreams is symbolic, it is personal to the dreamer. The way a dream is organized or comes together is unique to each person. Each dreamer has a personal associative meaning to each symbol in their dream and in their waking life. This is why it's beneficial to ask yourself what the sequence of events in a dream mean to you. Until you become adept at being a conscious dreamer, this is how you can discern your own messages from your own symbolism.

Q. Can I dream in French or Swahili if I speak only English?

A. You don't dream in a foreign language because you have created a symbolic association with your dominant language, which is the language that your subconscious uses to convey messages to you. This is not to say that you couldn't have a dream where you are speaking a different language!

In these cases, the message would most likely mean you lived a life in that language. In the waking state you would have to know that language in order to discern the message. However, it is likely your emotional body will have interpreted it anyway.

Chinese or Russians dream in their own languages because that is the language in which they associate the events in their lives. If you want to dream in Swahili, ask to dream in Swahili.

Q. Believers in Jesus seem to dream of the image of Jesus they grew up with, whereas other cultures will have grown up with different images. Since no one can prove what Jesus looked like, are we making up our own associations and that is what appears to us?

A. Yes, this is true, but remember, one of the *purposes* of dreams is to get a message across, which is why dream language is so personal. It's all about association.

I had a friend once who was not very spiritual. His dad had passed away and I happened to meet with him at a shop that I owned. He told me he had a very strange dream where his dad appeared to him and said, "I am perceived only by you." He was a bit confused about what that actually meant, but it makes the point that much of our imagery of people, places and things is relative only to us in our own minds.

Another example is when you tune into someone who has died. They will appear very much as they did in their Earth life, perhaps younger at times, or more radiant, but still with the same basic face or body appearance as when they were physically alive. Do they look like that once they're in spirit? It's possible, but they may appear a certain way to reassure family and friends still on Earth.

Q. *Can you ask any question, or ask for a vision in a dream?*

A. Yes. You can ask for insight, clarity, inspiration—anything.

Q. *How can I help patients who share their dreams with me?*

A. You can encourage them to be conscious dreamers because it is really important for people to establish their own language for their own dreams. This will empower them on a personal level to be able to decipher what their own dreams are telling them. It is also important for us not to interpret others' dreams, but rather to encourage them to describe what their own dreams mean to them.

Remember, everybody has an associative mind and we each know what things mean to us personally. It's just a matter of inquiry and taking the time to sit and feel what the scenario in a dream might feel like, or what it may mean symbolically. The reason it's so important to encourage more conscious dreaming or even to encourage someone to examine the meaning of their own dreams is so they can monitor their own personal progress in their lives and get very clear on what their choices are.

If you were to encourage your patients to do this and keep a notebook, they can then bring you the results of their own interpretations and in so doing, you would be better able to know how to help them. It would be a co-creative interaction between your patient and yourself. You would also be able to offer your own insights at that point. You would be having a lively discussion about what feels right or what other options are for their lives. In this way, both of you would be coming from a place of strength where neither one has authority over the other. You would be helping to co-create the highest possible outcome for both your patient and yourself. It is important that we be careful not to put our own language into another person's dreams, but rather help them discover their own language through their own inquiry. You can then repeat back to them what they are sharing with you about their own interpretations so they can hear it and decide if it feels right or accurate to them, which will allow them to strengthen their own communication language with themselves.

Q. *Does a separate consciousness do all the creating, or does consciousness interrelate with other dimensional levels to cause a co-creative experience?*

A. It is more that we are relating with the field of 'All That Is', which is interacting with us and manifesting our thoughts and reflecting them back to us. In other words, conscious creation is a co-creative endeavor because everything is alive as consciousness, therefore everything is always interrelating with everything else. The thing about becoming a conscious creator is that you *consciously* interact with the field of 'All That Is, which can cause a very different type of co-creative relationship with the intelligence of all life. The only reason that things seem to be going on without our conscious awareness is simply because we are not directing our attention to the relationship we have with all life everywhere.

* * *

Q. *There are many books and interpretations about dreams, Jungian, Freudian and metaphysical. Are you saying that none of them are beneficial? Is any one better than the other?*

A. It isn't that one is better than the other or some more accurate than others. There may be interpretations of dreams that resonate with a person when they are trying to find their associations within their own dreams. For example, I have gone through periods in my life when I resonated with certain books or other people's opinions about dreams. Later, as I grew and evolved, those same books stopped resonating with me. Eventually, I realized I was my own best interpreter of my dreams. Whatever people need at their own level of consciousness to help them decipher their own language is best for them at the time, for as long as it serves them. Some people are attracted to the Jungian interpretations of archetypes and the collective unconscious, while others are attracted to the Freudian sexuality symbolism. Another may go into the Shamanism version of the Dreamtime. Perhaps none of those apply, which is why ultimately your own symbolic language is best.

Q. *When we wake up, the dream disappears and we have no recollection of it. Does the dream sphere disappear, too?*

A. Every thought form has existence on some level. Whether it dissipates or is attracted to a thought form stronger than itself depends upon how much it is energized or what is in close proximity to it. These factors determine whether the thought form becomes a thing in and of itself or dissolves into nothing.

Much of the reason people don't remember their dreams is because as they wake up, a different part of their brain switches on due to the sunrise—different chemicals are released in the brain as daylight ensues. As you awaken, an entirely different hormonal process begins. The brain has already begun to switch modes and the events of the night have been put into the background.

As mentioned earlier, some dreams are designed to process events of the day and others for replenishing the colors in our bodies and physical systems. When you have a message dream, it will most likely gnaw at you throughout the day, or you will remember it soon after you awake, which is why it is good to have a notebook and pen nearby so you can write down your dream before you get too involved in your 3D activities.

Q. *Do people who have crossed over dream?*

A. They have no need—they are already in the spirit world.

Q. *Can dreams foretell the future? What are prophetic dreams?*

A. Prophetic dreams are probable realities that are floating around in the mass consciousness. They will always have a resonance with the person who is doing the dreaming. In other words, there is something about the person that resonates with the prophecy on some level. We can actually help a negative prophecy dream manifest by becoming emotionally involved in its scenario. By doing this, we inadvertently energize it.

I had a dream a couple of months ago that the financial system had collapsed, everyone was scattered and there was chaos everywhere. In the dream, we were living in a very tall, white, high-rise. When we heard the news we went downstairs and everything was covered with a gray ash, like a nuclear winter. Two store owners gave Ahonu and I packages of food that had to be mixed with water. They gave them to us for free as there was no water to be found anywhere. I woke up horrified because it felt like something was going to happen soon. I was feeling the emotion of impending doom. I got a hold of myself and reminded myself that I was looking at a *possible* future and not an *absolute* future. Once I realized this, I said No to the scenario and chose peace instead. Immediately, I regained feelings of peace and safety. In this way, I didn't give any more energy to the negative potential future.

Sometimes people dream of scenarios that are occurring in the present. This happened to me once when I was dreaming about a plane crash near a small island. I was watching the small plane fall down into the water. There were other people around on the island who seem to be involved somehow in this crash. The next day the news covered the plane crash of John Kennedy, Jr. off the coast of Martha's Vineyard. In that case, I was dreaming about something that was occurring at the moment I was dreaming. This was a case where I intercepted the same timeline as John Jr.'s timeline and was an observer in the situation.

People who dream of disasters seem to like it when their dreams come true, If you talk to people who continually dream of things that come true, you will find that most often they are dreaming of someone dying or of some disaster. These people may think that they are really psychic and able to tune into the future, but what is most likely happening is that they are being used by dark forces to help manifest those probabilities. We need to remember how powerful our minds are. Every thought takes form on some level. We need to be more conscious of what kinds of thoughts and visuals we are giving our energy and emotion to.

When you dream, you can tune into many possible future timelines. No one is more psychic than anyone else in this process. We all travel to different probabilities when we dream. It is valuable for us to become conscious creators in the dream state so that we can defer negative dream probabilities and replace them with better outcomes. In other words, be a creator of miraculous futures instead of catastrophes. The frequencies that we broadcast across the nerve network in our solar plexus determine what we help manifest in our world. We are all affected by what we collectively contribute energetically. We are all connected to each other through the nerve network in our solar plexus, which connects to the grids around the Earth. Walk away from fear and choose to broadcast miracle scenarios across the Earth's electro-magnetic grid.

* * *

Q. *Do dreamcatchers really keep negative spirits out?*

A. Dreamcatchers are talismans. Talismans are objects that are made or used in rituals that are imbued with particular meanings, geometries or intentions for a desired outcome. A talisman can be very powerful depending upon the intention that's put into it and the ancient history that it holds. Dreamcatchers can help keep negative spirits out because they have an ancient ancestry connected to them as symbols of power and protection. Dreamcatchers carry a particular vibrational frequency that can offer an energy of protection based on its original intention.

Q. *Are our dreams being influenced by the current cycle?*

A. I'm hearing the gap or barrier between the spirit world and our 3D world is thinning. Because of this, we have access to many other dimensions in our dream state that would have been difficult to reach previously. The consequences are that you can manifest faster, which applies to positive as well as negative. Another reason to be miracle minded!

Q. *Is it possible to collaborate with other people in our dreams? In other words, could you decide to get together with someone before you each go to sleep and decide to meet each other in a dream for a specific purpose or to do some manifesting?*

A. You could definitely do that! It would be a great experiment. You could even make an agreement to arrange to meet certain geniuses who have passed on to obtain knowledge about a particular subject if they are willing! You can also make arrangements to meet people who can give you information about healing the Earth or breaking through perceived barriers or limitations. These are just a few suggestions. You can start your own dream group!

* * *

Q. *Do I need the consent of another to meet them in a dream?*

A. Yes, you do, if you are talking about doing an experiment with a friend who is in 3D with you. You can't collaborate with others without their knowledge. How would it be a team experiment if you didn't agree to meet the other person first?

Q. *Can we use dreams to meet relatives who have crossed over?*

A. Yes, but first ask if they are available to meet with you and then make sure you have a good reason for calling them in. This is really a good procedure with whomever you may decide to communicate with.

One night many years ago, I went out of my body, but was not in the dream state. I decided to go see what this guy was doing that I was interested in. It was about 3 a.m. I immediately went to where he was—at a friend's house with a group of other people. I could see through the walls of the house and I could see him walking back and forth from his van to the house, possibly smoking pot. I was only watching this for a moment when I was put back into my body by my Guides who gave me a very strong message that spying on someone else when I was out of my body was a 'no-no'. So, you get the point.

Participant: *"I knew a homeopath who had conversations with Samuel Hahnemann, the founder of Homeopathy, in her dreams. She did this by taking remedies that allowed her to have conversations with people who had passed on. There were things she disagreed with him on and she told him so!"*

Q. *When a person has a sexual dream with another person, is that collaboration? If not, what is going on there?*

A. Obviously, if they're having a sexual dream involving another person, it's likely there is an agreement on some level between the people involved. There's no judgment in it.

When they awaken, they could ask what its meaning or purpose was for them. They might be attracting an entity to themselves that is not in their best interest, or the dream may reflect a fantasy, or some unfulfilled part of themselves.

Sexual experiences in dreams reflect unfulfilled desires, although some are unions with other energies, depending on what they symbolize. Bringing this full circle to the realization that everybody in a dream is an aspect of themselves suggests they could learn much by knowing themselves more deeply.

Q. *Are sleep dreams the same as daydreams?*

A. No, daydreams are either fantasies or imagination, which is not the same as the process of sleep dreaming. In daydreams, your consciousness isn't actually going to different frequency bands or dimensions. People who daydream are taking their focus away from their current physical reality and going into their imagination. A daydream can also be an inspired creation being received from Higher Guidance. You're not in the dream state when this is happening in your waking life.

Q. *Could we daydream for a positive outcome?*

A. Instead of that, imagine a world in which everyone is in the flow of their true creative power. Someone in the flow of their own creative power would naturally be creating positive futures and outcomes moment-to-moment. As we become more in the flow of Love's natural creative presence, beautiful futures naturally follow. Being in Love's flow reinforces everyone's divine genius and allows them their own creative expressions.

Q. *Does reinforcing my divine genius reinforce it for all?*

A. On a collective level, everything you do affects the whole. If you reinforce your own genius, it is an accomplishment that makes it vibrationally possible for everyone to do the same. You can't do it *for* another person, but you are strengthening the potential timeline in the collective field. You're contributing to the pool in which divine genius is manifesting on Earth.

Q. *Are there effects from being woken from a dream?*

A. It may cause a cascade of hormones in the shock of waking from one reality into another. The body will put things back in rhythm before too long. However, there are times when you may feel off for a time before you come fully back into your body.

Q. *What do flying dreams, being chased or falling mean?*

A. Flying is the natural state you're in when dreaming. It is what happens when you're temporarily free of your body. Dreams in which you are being chased usually have to do with subconscious fears you haven't cleared yet. These dreams show you what the fear is, especially if they're recurring. They could be about a demon or some other entity attachment. They can also represent you trying to run away from something in your everyday life or from something much deeper.

Dreams of falling are dreams in which you feel out of control in some aspect of your life. They may represent issues of safety, security and trust. Often in these of dreams, someone will either wake up before they actually land or they will land but land softly, showing the danger they perceived was not as bad or real as they thought. If you were to wake up in this type of dream before you actually land, it might show you that you're not ready to face whatever the perceived danger or threat is.

Q. *Must you be comfortable in bed to have lucid dreams?*

A. It has more to do with where the brain is at the time and what frequencies are running through it. In other words, the brainwave activity determines what types of dreams are unfolding in your consciousness. I'm also being told that hormone levels determine what types of openings the brain can access during sleep. In other words, are you in a light sleep or deep sleep? Hormones and the chemicals they produce, and Grid conditions have a lot to do with our state of enlightenment.

If you deliberately make a practice of Lucid Dreaming, the chemicals and hormones you produce while sleeping will change. Remember also, each hormone and the chemicals in them contain colors. Hormones are like keys that unlock doorways that create openings in the brain. Whatever you focus on determines what types of chemicals and hormones you produce. However, if you make it a deliberate practice to establish communication with different parts of yourself or your higher parts, your consciousness will listen to you and begin to produce the types of hormones and chemicals you need to accomplish your desire. It is always preferable that your state of consciousness be formed by your own conscious will and intention.

Q. *What are nightmares?*

A. Nightmares are an interface between a fear and a dimensional reality that matches it. They can be produced when hormones are out of balance, but most nightmares can be traced back to the quality of the person's thoughts or to their diet.

Q. *How can we protect our dream state?*

A. Bring your Guardian Angel into your dream state with you or your own I AM Presence. Do this by consciously inviting them into your sleep state before you go to bed. We need to remember that our Guardian Angel is a powerful presence that gets appointed to each of us individually to help us complete our soul contract. It has tremendous power to help, protect and intercede to help us fulfill our purpose. Having a more conscious relationship with It can propel us forward in many ways. In the end, it's all about our own self-mastery.

Chapter Eleven

The Brain

The Brain

Aingeal: "As I said the opening prayer, the room filled with the familiar red light that oftentimes accompanies topics that have to do with the physical world."

Q. *Why does the brain have two separate hemispheres?*

A. The answer that I'm hearing is that the brain actually *doesn't* have two separate hemispheres. The two hemispheres of the brain send signals back and forth to each other, but they don't perceive themselves as separate hemispheres. They don't want us to perceive them that way. I see them functioning together. There are myriads of electronic signals passing back and forth between them constantly.

They each may take on a different *job*, but they don't want to be thought of as separate. They work in harmony with one another and they complement each other, even to the point of restoring a deficiency in one part. We can't make a general statement that one hemisphere does only one thing and the other does another. For example, if you remove one hemisphere or part of one hemisphere, the other hemisphere will naturally take on the function of what is missing.

The brain is telling me that it wants to be called a *being*, because it is the connector between your Individuated Spirit, the Mind Field and the Body. The brain is a *receiving and transmitting station* that seems to have a consciousness of its own.

It wants to be called a *being* because it is vibrantly aware. The brain is where the Individuated Spirit and the Mind Field interface with the Body.

When I look at the brain, I do not see it as solid, but rather as a hollow sphere of light. I see *through* it. I do not get a sense of denseness. It appears *translucent*, with electrical firings going on back and forth. The brain relays the beliefs and thoughts of the Individuated Spirit and the Mind Field to the Body.

Even though we think the brain is the main intelligence, the brain wouldn't necessarily agree with that. It is the receiving station or hub for the Spirit–Mind Field–Body complex and relays its information to the body and its organs, like the switchboard operators who used to connect our telephone calls by plugging wires into various openings.

When you look at switchboards you see various wires crisscrossing each other, which is similar to how these brain firings look. The brain is the main operator responsible for relaying signals and connections back and forth for a myriad of functions. You can also say it is a mass of highways that send and receive thought impulses or messages. The brain is also *non-local*, which means it can transmit and receive signals from and through the Universe, as well as to and from any stationary body.

Q. *Why does the brain look like it has separate lobes?*

A. It appears this way because different parts of it perform certain functions in the *overall process*. Functions dictate shape and size. One part would still cover for another, however, if a part gets damaged.

We had intended to go through all the different lobes of the brain, but the brain has its own agenda tonight! I'm being shown that all the lobes of the brain work together. If you try to isolate parts of the brain—let's say you try to put cells of the limbic system under a microscope, you wouldn't find any emotions in those cells.

In other words, you can't take parts of the brain apart and find the particular function that you think a part does. You won't find it physically or chemically, because it changes all the time. The brain stores certain chemicals in parts of it however, but even those chemicals are influenced by the Spirit and the Mind of the Individual Consciousness. We can assume that these chemicals are in a constant state of flux.

Even when these chemicals cascade through a physical body or *unit* as they are calling it, the whole field can still change in an instant depending on what's coming across. *The brain is a limitless relay station.* Anything can be produced in it, anything is possible in it and it can transfer changes across the fields of the body. It affects all the cells and organs instantaneously. The brain is controlled by the Spirit–Mind Field complex of the individual. The *quality* of that interaction has to do with the Individual Spirit and the Mind Field and how they are relating.

Q. *What happens if someone is permanently brain damaged?*

A. There is actually a disconnect happening with the Individuated Spirit in that it is *withdrawing* a huge portion of itself and becoming an *observer* rather than a *participator* in the Earth experience. The reasons are wide and varied for the Individuated Spirit having this experience.

Let's talk about the distinction between the Individuated Spirit and the Mind Field. The Individuated Spirit is the actual *identity* of the person, or the actual being. The Mind Field is the *substance* or *plasma* that turns the beliefs and conclusions of the Individuated Spirit into concepts.

The Individuated Spirit needs the Mind Field to transfer its beliefs about reality into words, concepts or ideas. The Mind Field is the substance that down-steps associations and turns them into concepts or ideas. The brain takes those concepts and turns them into electrical impulses, chemicals and hormones that are then relayed to the body of the Individuated Spirit.

We always thought that spirit is perfect, but I'm hearing that Individuated Spirits are all at different levels of evolution and awareness, different levels of maturity and benevolence, *etc*. Each Individuated Spirit is on its own journey of Self-Realization.

Spirits grow and evolve. They can also digress. As long as the Universe keeps expanding, so will the potential for Individuated Spirits to grow and expand into more Godliness.

The Mind Field is what allows Individuated Spirits to have experiences in dimensions of varying types. The substance of the Mind Field feels sticky. This entire process happens quite quickly —much more quickly than the time it's taking me to explain it.

The brain is explaining to me that it is an interface system—a relay or transmitting station. It of itself does not *cause* thoughts.

The purpose of having a body is so the Individuated Spirit can move around and have experiences in this dimension. Earth is a particular level of densification; therefore we need a vehicle in which we can stay long enough to do the things we set out to do. If you were to go into other dimensions or planes of existence that are not as dense, the type of body you would create would be very different. In some less dense dimensions you do not need a body at all, whereas in other denser ones, you may need an even denser body to survive. The same is true with respect to other planets and their life forms.

The density of our bodies also explains why disembodied spirits hang around us when they don't go into the light. They know that as a spirit, they cannot affect our dimension in any significant way. They may be able to knock things over or cause other poltergeist-like effects, but they themselves cannot maneuver themselves powerfully enough to still *live* in this dimension, which is why they often try to attach themselves to someone who is still alive here.

Q. *I'm surprised to find out that Individuated Spirits are not perfect. Could you go into this a little more?*

A. A good example is to think of stars. You can look up into the sky and see stars of all kinds of varying shapes and sizes. Some are huge, while others are medium sized or very small. Each star has its own momentum of power or influence, depending upon its size. Individuated Spirits are much like this in that they are not all created the same size or shape.

Some have more mass and influence, while others have much less. Smaller, or less mature spirits go through a process of evolution in which they may be pulled toward other spirits that are grander than themselves until they learn or evolve to the extent that they themselves become magnificent. You can see that Spirits have great potential to continue to grow and expand or burn out and die, much as stars do.

The *perfection* in all this is that each Spirit is made from the same lifeforce energy as every other Spirit. Therefore, it is unlimited in its capabilities for evolution throughout the Universe. The Spirit will down-step itself into various forms on various planets and dimensions to have experiences and grow, once it gains the ability to do so.

Q. *Could an Individuated Spirit in a body decide it does not want to ascend but rather stay Earthbound for many lifetimes?*

A. Yes, that's possible. It's why many people do not achieve ascension from Earth. When the Individuated Spirit gets to the point where it is self-realized enough in its consciousness, it will be done with the physical body experience and will move on. This is when it will go through a resurrection and ascension process.

Q. *So ascension has nothing to do with the mind, brain or body?*

A. That's right. Ascension is the condition of the Individuated Spirit and its consciousness. The consciousness affects all the levels below it. The problem we have with this dimension, is that once a portion of our spirit is incarnate into a body, we tend to forget that we are a Spirit who is here for experiences.

However, you eventually come to a place where you remember what you're doing here and your consciousness expands. Once you realize you are not just a body, you will turn your attention once again to your Spirit self. When this happens, your consciousness will change, grow and expand, until eventually it recognizes itself as one with all. You will also realize that it is *your* Spirit who is doing the observing, deciding and thinking.

Q. *Do we re-enact our perceived separation from Source each time we incarnate? Have we recreated the Fall here by taking on a Spirit–Mind–Brain–Body system?*

A. I'm not seeing it like that. Whether we have re-enacted the belief in separation or not, we can still return to the remembrance of our Spirit selves while in a physical body. I am saying this to avoid our falling into judgment and guilt about being physical. A part of our Spirit is within us—it gnaws at us to grow and realize ourselves which accounts for the restlessness and desire that we feel when it is time to grow further in our self-realization process.

Q. *So, if our Spirit is the thinker, observer and decider, do we ever realize that our relationship with Source is the key?*

A. The Individuated Spirit I am seeing, which *is* us, did not deliberately separate from Source. Spirits are born at different rates of vibration and states of awareness. I don't see us making any big decision to deliberately cut ourselves off from Source. Some of us are like pebbles on the beach and some of us are huge boulders. What you are and what frequency you vibrate at determines your journey, or evolution, through the Universe. The bigger your momentum, the more power you exert through this journey. When your self-awareness increases, you become a more conscious being until you become more and more God-Realized, which is the memory that you are light, sound and Love.

Keep in mind we are talking about a journey extending billions of years. You could be a small spark of the Creator and build your own momentum until you become a force to be reckoned with in and of yourself. Or, you could have been created as a spark, in which case you would have more individual momentum and force from the beginning. Regardless of which it is, everything in Creation will eventually become God-Realized through the various journeys it takes, the awareness it attains and the decisions it makes once it becomes self-aware.

An example is when people go to a psychic reader who tells them they are a young soul or an old soul—implying that you may be a young or immature spirit or a mature or older spirit.

If you look out into the world and see the diversity of people and all their different beliefs, thoughts and perceptions, it's easy to see they range from the most enslaved to the most free. It is evident that everyone is at a different place of self-awareness. Some people never gain much self-awareness or evolution of consciousness in a particular life or even after many lives, which is when they repeatedly return into the environment where they left off to give themselves the opportunity to grow once again.

Eventually, those with limited perceptions and dogmatic beliefs will question their beliefs and when this happens, they are on their way to the evolution of higher consciousness.

Then you will be aware enough and will have grown enough to say you are done with experiencing the physical Universe and its physical bodies, or that you're done with whatever planet you may have been experiencing. You will become so much like the Creator that you will want to merge with It. When that happens, you will be on an entirely new journey.

It is our Spirits that are learning, that are becoming greater and more self-aware and conscious. It is our Spirits that are on the journey of self-realization until they become *pure*. You could say our Individuated Spirits eventually become *Parent Spirits*, implying they have such a powerful creative life force of their own that they create more and more life.

* * *

Q. *A Spirit that would want to create a Mind–Brain–Body system would have to be in error, wouldn't it?*

A. No, of course not! Earth is one journey—somewhere else will be another. It is more about the level at which you were created. If you're a baby Spirit, you have to go through your stages of development to reach maturity. Not all Spirits are created equal. This is just the way it is—the way things come off Source—an infinite supply of sparks of God, each at a different frequency and vibration.

One evening many years ago, I was in a three-hour meditation in which I was shown all the sparks of light coming off Creator. Some were big, some were small, some were medium, *etc.* The larger ones carried more attractive energy than the others. The smaller and medium ones were being pulled in toward the larger ones, becoming part of them.

Every spark at some point will grow to become a Parent Sun. If you were a small spark with no larger bodies near you when you came off Source, you would continue on your evolutionary journey throughout the Universe.

This attraction goes on throughout the Universe. Some sparks pull things to them, while others repel them depending upon their make-up. The goal is for all sparks to become Parent Suns—in other words—*givers of life* unto themselves. Even if a spark takes on a *reverse* journey and ends up compacting in upon itself, it will still return to a universal element and begin again. It may go through various cycles in which it has no self-will until it becomes free. It doesn't matter how long it takes for an Individuated spark to become a Parent Sun/Son. All will eventually achieve self-consciousness and God-Realization.

Q. *What part of the brain signals pain?*

A. Give me a moment as I'm seeing the brain light up. It is showing me that it all functions together, not separately. Pain is the reaction of a person's consciousness to an event or experience.

There is an association made between the person's consciousness and what is happening to them that actually causes a pain reaction, which is why no one experiences pain the same way. Two people could have the same experience and each would come away with a personal association and conclusion about the experience. One person may find a situation painful while another person may not. It has a lot to do with how the individual consciousness processes the experience.

The body reacts to the pain stimulus from the consciousness of the individual. It is not the body that says it's in pain, but rather the consciousness inhabiting the body that *feels* the pain. When the body receives the pain signal, it immediately begins restoring balance as much as possible, *i.e.*, it *responds* to a message that is being sent to it via the Individuated consciousness. The Individuated Spirit projects its pain onto the body.

Q. *Can we control pain without drugs?*

A. Yes, pain can be controlled without drugs. The body itself reacts to pain signals immediately.

I don't see the body causing pain, but rather it reacts to pain, working to counterbalance the problem. The body immediately sends chemicals and hormones to the painful area to alleviate it or bring balance to it. It does not always bring relief because hormones and chemicals do not work the same in all bodies, depending upon their condition.

Q. *Does all pain have the same purpose?*

A. Pain on any level—physical, mental, emotional or spiritual—notifies the individual that something is happening to them or their world with which they are not in agreement or which they don't like. The feeler of the pain has an emotional reaction to something going on in their environment, which is actually where pain comes from. What's going on and how the person is *receiving* and *interpreting* it determines the *level* of pain.

Pain is common here in this dimension because so much happens here that registers as not okay with us. Pain is a signal in our consciousness that what is happening is not what we *want* to happen. Now that you know this, it is possible to help others look at what may be going on in their lives that is not sitting right with them. You would do this process individually, like homeopathy, where each person is treated as an individual with a personal set of symptoms. Pain can be a useful signal to help rebalance a person, but there is no general remedy for pain because each individual has a personal associative reaction. When someone tells you they are in pain, you can't really experience what they're feeling, because you, as another Individuated consciousness, experience reality in your own unique way.

At another level, someone can experience pain while going through a process of change or a shift from the old to the new. If you feel pain, it would be good practice to do some self-inquiry to see if your pain derives from associations or victim responses or if it comes from moving to a different level of consciousness.

In other words, are you stuck in the old, while things are changing in your life? The change could be physical, emotional, mental or spiritual. Self-inquiry into the pain will determine which it is. Pain can let you know that you need to make a change or that you are in a process of change. Conversely, when someone is at peace with their world they do not experience pain. The events in their world do not affect them the same way.

Q. *How do colors affect the brain?*

A. Colors break down into chemicals and hormones as sunlight comes in through the brain. These chemicals and hormones each have their own properties depending on the color.

Q. *Are Chakras colors?*

A. Chakras are vortices, not colors. They embody colors.

* * *

Q. *Is there a particular color related to each hormone?*

A. Hormones are a combination of colors and elements. For example, testosterone has a beautiful rosy plum purple color with a reddish hue and a hint of orange.

Q. *What colors relate to the hormones of the thyroid?*

A. People often assign blue to the thyroid, but I see gold, white and clear light with the texture of a light syrup.

Q. *How about pituitary hormones?*

A. I see a reddish-brown color with small amounts of different colors and I feel a pulsing as I tune into it. The red-brown color seems to be a result of a mixture of other colors. It has small amounts of green, orange, yellow and some violet. It actually may have all the rainbow colors mixed in small amounts.

Each hormone takes on a particular pattern as well as the colors. The pituitary, for example, appears as little rectangles and triangles and I am aware of a specifically organized geometric pattern. The thyroid appears as a chain, all linked together. Testosterone appears as a DNA chain, which leads me to believe that it may influence the DNA's structure or operation.

Q. *What colors relate to estrogen?*

A. I see pink, white, gold and a little blue. Chemically, it feels soft, loving and nurturing. It has a spherical shape.

Q. *What colors relate to the pineal gland?*

A. I see white and gold. On the outside it is rough, like a nut.

Q. *How about serotonin?*

* * *

A. I am seeing yellow—almost golden, but not quite. Around the outside of the chemical I see a small line of bluish purple that flows through the body, acting as a protector, like a guardian chemical. Imagine serotonin as a security guard checking everything to make sure everything is on or off as it should be. It goes through the body and makes sure everything is connected properly and functioning correctly. It switches things on and off as needed. It makes me feel positive and happy when I tune into it. It also feels like a lubricant as it goes through the body.

Q. *Melatonin?*

A. It has a rosy color—red-violet with some white. Melatonin seems to have a lot to do with cellular structure. I see a picture of little white cells. Melatonin seems to affect the quality of those cells—how awake they are, how well they can function. Even though melatonin has been known to be the chemical to help people sleep, I'm seeing that its function in the cells is actually to keep them awake and functioning properly.

Q. *How does the ego relate to perception?*

A. Remember that our Individuated Spirit is really the thinker having an experience with a particular level of awareness and dimension. We mistakenly think that we are a body with a brain that is doing the thinking. We think we are a *person* walking around in a physical body, which is a misperception because our Spirit's are really doing it all. We have defined who we think we are because we do not remember our Spirit self. This self-defined image is our *Alter-ego*—a false sense of identity. It is a self that is vulnerable to how it is seen and perceived. It makes itself up as it goes along. Sometimes it is grand, other times impoverished. Its sense of self changes depending on how it sees itself at any given moment or on how others see it.

It measures its success or failure on external happenings. None of this is the Spirit that is trying to learn in this dimension.

If you focus only at the body level, you will perceive God and Spirit as up and distant, while the truth is that a portion of your Individuated Spirit has come *down* into this level. The alter-ego self that is here believing that it is the thinker is in error.

Once you're down here and functioning only at the horizontal or linear level—you walk horizontally, you perceive horizontally—that makes you think that you are a linear identity, what we call the alter-ego identity. The alter-ego isn't wrong, it's just incomplete, so it doesn't recognize itself as an Individuated Spirit learning to become Self-realized. The alter-ego self is vulnerable to being torn down or built up, influenced by others and subjected to attack from the outside. It is also subject to disease and death *because* of how it sees itself.

Spirit is spherical. Being in the *now* is a spherical action. It is moment-to-moment with each moment complete in and of itself. It's not thinking about the past, present or future, which are all linear perspectives. Our particular orientation determines whether we are in our alter-ego identification or our Spirit identification. *Waking up* is when you realize the difference.

Q. *What does Source have to say about memory?*

A. I am seeing violet-purple. Memory is nonlocal—it is everywhere and in every cell—not restricted to the brain. However, there is a *function* of the brain that can *locate* memories. The brain has the ability to call a memory forth and translate it to you visually, mentally or emotionally. It is a mediator with an unlimited capability to receive, transmit, send signals and ideas. It can also locate a point in outer space if you tell it to. It could find it and transmit that information to you. The brain in and of itself does not hold on to anything.

Q. *How does something become a memory?*

A. Memory is the *incorporation of an experience* into the consciousness of the Individuated Spirit.

Q. *What is logical thinking?*

A. *All* thinking comes from your Individuated Spirit. So when you say 'Logical', it all depends upon what Spirit is thinking at any given point or what it wants. In other words, if I want to *reason*, I will activate my ability to reason. My Spirit sends that message to the Mind Field and it says, "Okay, I'll organize that for you." The brain then goes ahead and produces the chemicals to allow that message to translate into a function. It's the same if your Spirit wanted to be creative rather than logical—it goes through the same downstepping process from the Individuated Spirit.

When people say the mind is all-powerful, they stop there and don't go any further. They don't realize that it isn't the mind, it is the Individuated Spirit that is thinking, observing and deciding. What is incredible about the Mind Field, is that it can take any thought, conclusion or association and turn it into a concept, thought-form or idea. It can take anything and turn it into something else. The Spirit's request does not always have to do with the body. It may desire to manifest a new house, for example. The Mind Field will take that desire and turn it into an organized pattern that has the potential to manifest in 3D.

Q. *How does the process of manifesting a desire work?*

A. This is so interesting—this process actually does involve the brain. The condition of the Individuated Spirit dictates what can manifest because Spirits are at all different levels of awareness. If the Individuated Spirit is trying to manifest a desire but is limited in its ideas or associations about reality at the subconscious level, it won't materialize certain things, because *the chemicals won't be produced to bring that desire into materialization.* In other words, the *magnetic field* that is needed to materialize a desire won't be produced, which implies that the *quality* of our thoughts and beliefs determines what chemicals and hormones are created. These in turn generate an appropriate magnetic field.

If the generated magnetic field isn't powerful enough, it won't manifest your desire, which is why you must determine the condition of your Spirit and what it has decided or assumed to be true. The condition of your Individuated Spirit determines what you can actualize in this dimension, which explains why some people's ability to manifest their desires seems limited or even thwarted. It also explains why some people end up with certain conditions or illnesses. Healing has to occur at the level of the Individuated Spirit because that is where ideas, conclusions, associations and programs originate.

Once you start to examine the condition of your own Spirit, you can then make different choices. Now that we know that our Individuated Spirit has limitations, we can also go to our I AM Presence for correction. (I'm experiencing heat in my body as I'm talking about this.) The Individuated Spirit itself needs a different message for correction from higher up. The change for any healing has to occur at the level *above* the Individuated Spirit first, so it can filter down to the other levels. This is to allow for more pure thought and perception to be received by the Individuated Spirit, which then gets conceptualized in the Mind Field, received by the brain and turned into chemicals and hormones for the body system, generating a new magnetic field. In effect, an entire new channel is opening. It can't work from the body up because it will not be a permanent correction. You can see that modalities that work to make changes below the level of Spirit will only produce a temporary correction until the Spirit itself gets healed.

The Individuated Spirit can and does have its own capacities for creative imagination but if there is trauma or damage at the level of the Individuated Spirit, its capacity to imagine and be creative will be thwarted. Once it realizes that it's being confronted with its own limitations, it can then ask for help from a higher source. The ability to arrive at an awareness of one's own limitations is a spiritual evolution. The very fact that we have come to this awareness shows us something is working within us to take us to a higher level.

Q. What is perception?

A. When the Individuated Spirit sends its thoughts to the Mind Field, the Mind Field makes a perception or *concept*, which is a way to orient ourselves as we move about our world.

Q. So, is perception a way to communicate?

A. Perception is an *effect* of the Mind Field turning thoughts and ideas into concepts. The Individuated Spirit uses perception to get concepts and thoughts across to others in a particular reality system. Perception only has the meaning you give it. In other words, your perceptions could be very different than another person's perceptions, depending upon the conclusions your own spirit has come to and how it sees and uses this reality. You can use your body to communicate verbally; you can communicate telepathically amongst yourselves and you can communicate Spirit to Spirit without using the body at all.

Q. Do we need to be consciously aware of communicating at these levels?

A. No. You are actually communicating with all life everywhere all the time whether you're consciously aware of it or not. All thoughts go into the Mind Field and get formed at varying levels. Being aware consciously only matters when you are communicating with something or someone deliberately. All thoughts float around in the Mind Field continually, including higher thoughts from higher beings as well as low thoughts from lower beings.

However, the ability to *receive* these thoughts depends entirely upon the individuals' orientation and perception of their reality and the condition of their brain. There are many people today who still can't understand mental telepathy or psychic awareness. They don't believe in it which puts a huge block to their ability to receive thoughts from the Mind Field.

Q. *How do you receive the information you get from Source?*

A. I receive it through and by Love's Presence. I feel and receive the information in every part of me.

Q. *As a Homeopath, part of what I encounter is the degree to which I can access the patient's Individuated Spirit self to see what condition it's in. Would the person's Spirit self be ready to be healed if it has come to so many conclusions about itself? Should I inquire at the level of the person's Spirit self?*

A. Yes, that's correct. A healer who can check a person's Individuated Spirit would also be able to see the Higher Spirit come in when the healer is asking for the solution. It is the higher being that brings forth a solution and knows exactly what the Individuated Spirit can accept and integrate. I'm getting the feeling that the higher being that comes forward is either a higher aspect of the Individuated Spirit itself, a Guide, an aspect of Source Itself, or the person's own I AM Presence. It would be a higher source connected to the Individuated Spirit and not some alien or being who has no connection or relationship to the individual. As a healer, your part is easy. You act as the mediator between the Individuated Spirit of your patient and the Higher Spirit who will come in to help the client.

Individuated Spirits are at various levels of awareness and evolution and because the Spirit is both the thinker and decider, it needs to actively participate in its own healing process. For example, it needs to be *willing* to have you check on the condition of itself first. Once you receive the information about their Spirit, you can see what the choices are for healing and you can present these choices to them. If they decide they desire the healing, you then call on their I AM Self to remove the damage or limitation in the Individuated Spirit. Your client should be able to feel the effects of this right away on some level. The effects may continue to be active for weeks or months and they can be reinforced with your homeopathic remedies, if needed.

Q. *Do I need to get permission from a client who's not progressing to ask their Individuated Spirit for more information?*

A. Yes, you do. This would be a great help to your patient, because until you can get answers from this level, you won't really know what is involved or what is really needed.

Technique for Healing: Once you have permission, close your eyes and focus on the person's Individuated Spirit by making the request to view it. Just take a look at it and observe it at first. See what condition it's in or what it may choose to impart to you. It may communicate with you through a picture of itself, it may say something verbally or it may impart a feeling or some other sensation. Once you feel you have a good assessment of its condition, you then call forth the higher being in charge of the person and ask it to heal the Individuated Spirit's condition. It will begin to do this immediately. You will be acting as the observer as this happens. You will also see when the healing is finished and how your client reacts to this process.

Unless you involve the patient's spiritual condition, trying to heal things from the level of the alter-ego or the mind level is never-ending.

Remember that the alter-ego is a false sense of identity that is predominantly linear in its approach to life. The alter-ego is also below the Mind level that conceptualizes everything. The alter-ego is a false identity that is wedded to the perception that we are just a body. It takes thoughts from the Mind Field and decides what parts it likes and makes a self that is fashioned after those ideas—it makes up a story about itself. It focuses horizontally and linearly, which is why it feels disconnected and separate, because it is. It hasn't the awareness of the Spirit self. The alter-ego, being a false sense of identity, actually blocks out Spirit's impulses. In contrast, the communication with the Individuated Spirit and its higher aspects is a *spherical* process that occurs moment to moment.

* * *

Q. *Is the alter-ego the self that is in time?*

A. Yes and no. It is in time because it is a self that was made while in a body and which perceives itself to be in time. However, the construct of time is invented by us and our perceptions.

Q. *What types of things inhibit the brain's ability to receive?*

A. Thoughts, perceptions, beliefs, personal traumas, the brain's physical condition, pollution, food quality, grid conditions where you live, EMF'S—all have a lot to do with the functions of the human brain. Chemicals and toxins that you consume through food and breathing affect the brain's functioning. I see a picture of wires being frayed or nerve endings becoming dehydrated, brittle and dry. For the brain to receive and deliver messages, it needs its electrical and nervous system to be in tip-top shape. The condition of the nasal passages also affects the brain—many toxins and poisons come in through the nose and are held in the sinus cavity.

This effect is secondary to what we've discussed earlier about the beliefs and programs of the Individuated Spirit that also limit what the brain can receive and send across to the body. To help combat these environmental effects, we need to be aware that the body needs an ample supply of good fats for its nervous system and brain to function. We recommend using organic coconut oil as food or in capsule form. We do ourselves a disservice by consuming low-fat foods, which can actually be a cause of memory loss and malfunctions in the brain. We also need adequate supplies of minerals and amino acids.

There are exercises that can be done to increase brain wiring which will go a long way to enhance the brain's ability to receive and transmit signals. See BrainHighways.com for info.

Q. *What can you advise for patients with Alzheimer's?*

A. I see heavy metal toxicity in the brain. There are also dehydration factors involved. So, we are looking for a good detoxification process for heavy metals, and we recommend frequent detoxification in general. The person's fat intake needs to be increased; we mentioned pure organic coconut oil as being a good source of fat. The person's diet needs to change to incorporate more raw and pure foods and more healthy fats. With Alzheimer's, sometimes the soul wants time to go back and forth between spirit life and earth life before it makes its transition. This is part of the progression you see with Alzheimer's patients where they progressively are 'gone' from this reality for longer periods of time and present for shorter periods.

Years of breathing polluted air, ingesting metals through food, amalgam fillings and even food preparation using aluminum pans, can all contribute to the buildup of heavy metals. For people with Alzheimer's this makes the brain look like it's suffocating from poor oxygen flow, therefore signals are not being sent across and the basic functioning of the brain deteriorates.

Conclusion

We began our journey exploring God and Its Creation. We found God and Love are one and the same and we have nothing to fear. We caught a glimpse of the vastness of Creation and its ever expanding potential. We found we each have an intimate place in it and we are all valuable beyond imagination. As we moved down the levels, we discovered the levels of consciousness and self-awareness and how they can be expressed. We found the role higher beings play in our lives and we gained an understanding of Love. We saw that Miracles happen by and through Love.

We extended this understanding into time-space and began to see how the template of original creation patterns Itself through all levels from the spiritual dimensions to the densification into form. It looks after us in our dreams and sustains us while we perceive ourselves so far from Home. At every level, there is a ladder taking us up, out and in, ensuring our safety on our journey. The same light and Love that is Source coalesces into an array of colors and music to form our bodies as we shape ourselves with our consciousness. Its life impulses beat our hearts, Its breath is our rhythm, Its aliveness carries on our body functions while we play with Creation.

And then one day we come to it—we wake up and remember we are *It*, the I AM. The memory was there all along, through every lifetime and dimension. It is everywhere, in our hearts and minds, in our bodies as the sleeping flame of Kundalini waiting to be awakened, waiting to ascend the ladder Home. Spiraling through the Chakra wheels, dancing in celebration, arriving, purifying, becoming... alive.

About The Author

Aingeal (Ann-gail) Rose O'Grady was born on November 11th, 1953 in Plattsburgh, New York. Her heart's desire when she was young was to marry and raise children. She fulfilled that dream with her three beautiful children, Clayton, Brooke and Janai and her delightful granddaughters, Grace Rose, Morgan Emma and Abby Quinn.

Aingeal's spiritual journey began when she was 19 following the tragic death of her first husband three months after their wedding. She dedicated herself to finding the answers to the deepest spiritual questions by journeying into the mysteries of the spirit, while exploring consciousness and its expansive potential. She spent years meditating and being taught by Archangel Raphael, who took her on journeys into other worlds and planes of existence. She went on to study the works of J. Kristnamurti, Sondra Ray, *The Science of Mind* and *A Course in Miracles*.

For more than twenty-five years she acquired certifications in numerous healing modalities, growing a thriving practice in Schaumburg, Illinois, always striving to help her clients and students achieve self-mastery. As a Tarot teacher and reader, she has taught and read for thousands of people on both sides of the Atlantic. She reads the Akashic Records privately for clients. Readings can be ordered from her website: aingealrose.com. She holds spiritually focused Akashic Group Sessions online from San Diego, California and Ireland. These Group Akashic Sessions, which focus on questions of a universal rather than a personal nature, form the backbone of the answers in this book.

She has been interviewed on radio shows worldwide including Coast-to-Coast AM with George Noory. She and her Twin Flame husband, Ahonu, present weekly podcasts on spirituality at: https://podcasts.worldofempowerment.com. Aingeal also makes one-of-a-kind handmade Fairies for customers worldwide.

As a seasoned spiritual teacher, Aingeal delights in facilitating the awakening of consciousness in her clients and students. Personal freedom, realizing the God Within, loving and respecting all life everywhere is the goal. Today Aingeal continues to teach *How To Read the Akashic Records*, *Transformational Writing*, the *Tarot, Beginning, Intermediate and Advanced* as well as *Healing with the Tarot*. Books she has written include *Tarot for Beginners, Love, Miracles & Original Creation, The Nature of Reality* and *Answers from the Akashic Records Vol 1-100*.

All books are available on Amazon.com and wherever fine books are sold. She can be contacted at: https://aingealrose.com.

All publishing inquiries to: admin@twinflameproductions.us

BIBLIOGRAPHY

Ahonu (2020). *Ahonu Visionary Artist.* From: https://ahonu.com
Brain Highways. *Fun, educational programs to improve learning, focus, and behavior.* https://www.BrainHighways.com
ECCH (2009). *The Legal Situation for the Practice of Homeopathy in Europe.* Retrieved from Scribd: https://bit.ly/legal-homeopathy
Melchizedek, Drunvalo. *The Ancient Secret of the Flower of Life, Vols. I & II.* From Amazon: https://amzn.to/317z3B3
O'Grady, Aingeal Rose. *A Time of Change.* Published by World of Empowerment: https://links.ahonu.com/atoc
O'Grady, Aingeal Rose. *Answers From The Akashic Records.* Published by World of Empowerment: https://links.ahonu.com/aftar
The Foundation For Inner Peace. *A Course In Miracles.* https://acim.org
Wikipedia. (2012, April 14). *Samuel Hahnemann—Founder of Homeopathy.* Retrieved from Wikipedia: http://tinyurl.com/27572n

Index

A
abundance 43-44, 59, 98
Akashic Records 10-13, 166
Angels 137-146, 149-151, 154,
animals 41, 61, 70, 89-90, 134, 148, 168, 202, 211
Armageddon 132-133
Ascension 48, 51, 55, 66, 76, 169-171, 192, 242
aura 160, 167-168

B
brain 3-5, 41, 45, 53, 67, 77-78, 81, 98, 120, 209-211, 216, 229, 235-245, 247, 249-253, 256-257

C
cancer 133, 174, 196
Christ 65
climate change 133
cosmic 33, 58, 65, 74, 171-172
cosmos 23, 35, 47, 52, 61, 74, 108, 135, 170

D
density, densification 5, 25, 90, 127, 139, 168, 200, 212, 241
DNA 31-47, 70, 74, 76, 82, 135, 248

E
ego 4, 8, 9, 35, 57, 85-87, 91-92, 96, 98, 100-102, 141, 249, 250, 255-256
Egypt 7
ETs 220
Evil 23, 39, 157-158, 179, 180, 182-184, 217-218, 220
Evolution 5, 6, 28, 32-37, 39-42, 44-46, 49, 60, 65, 70, 73, 102, 135, 154, 171, 174, 241-244, 252, 254
extraterrestrials See ETs

F
fall, the 243
forgiveness 38-39, 50, 96, 155, 186-187, 193, 196, 199

G
GMO 45
golden, gold 6-7, 48, 106, 207, 248
H
harmonic, harmonics 55, 63
health 61, 62, 75, 88, 140, 169
Heaven 6, 181, 225
Homeopathy 233, 247, 262
human, humanity 7, 21-22, 24, 33-36, 38, 40-41, 43, 46, 56, 74, 89, 129, 161, 164, 168, 201, 204, 211, 256
I
incarnate, incarnation, reincarnation 13, 41-42, 51, 56, 73, 79, 81, 92-93, 142, 158, 242-243
individuated spirit 4-5, 8-9, 14, 56, 78, 238-244, 246, 249, 250-256
intuition 57, 202
J
Jesus 20, 26, 38-39, 100, 141, 190, 191, 226
joy 28, 30, 100, 101, 121, 125, 162, 189
K
Karma 37-39, 51, 112, 122, 140
L
love—this book is full of love with too many individual entries to list here
M
meditation 79, 99-100, 127, 134, 149, 207, 245
money 97-98, 130, 190
mother 63-64, 78, 157, 196, 205
O
organic 45, 85, 256-257
P
prayer 11, 18, 24-26, 29, 48, 66, 84, 106, 122, 138, 160, 199, 238
prosperity, prosperous 48, 59, 98, 199
psychic 13, 46, 59, 69, 134, 166-167, 188, 231, 244, 253
R
rainbow 135, 248
reincarnation See Incarnation
Resurrection 38, 76, 242
S
sleep 114, 209-210, 213-214, 216, 218, 223-224, 232, 234, 236, 249
T
technology 117, 154, 165

telepathy, telepathic 10, 33, 69, 99, 142, 154, 194, 253
trees 43, 102, 150, 199
trauma 4, 8, 62, 72, 75, 115, 120, 126, 135, 148, 252, 256
Twin Flames 42, 261
U
Universe 4, 7, 13, 15, 22-23, 32, 51-52, 54-56, 59, 70, 91, 97, 102, 113, 116, 163, 170, 177, 184, 191, 214, 239, 241-245, 260
W
water 62, 118, 119, 120, 128, 149, 150, 165, 182, 230-231

Thank you!

Also read *A Time Of Change*
https://atimeofchange.info

Followed by Volumes 1-100 of
Answers From The Akashic Records
https://answersfromtheakashicrecords.com

Details of all books/workshops/courses from
https://aingealrose.com

Aingeal Rose

CPSIA information can be obtained
at www.ICGtesting.com
Printed in the USA
LVHW052357040323
740850LV00007B/64

Love, Miracles & Original Creation

*Spiritual Guidance
for Understanding Life and Its Purpose*

Aingeal Rose O'Grady

Copyright © 2021 Aingeal Rose

All rights reserved. No part of this book may be reproduced in any form or by any electronic or mechanical means including information and retrieval systems without prior permission from the publisher in writing.

Library of Congress Cataloging-in-Publication Data
O'Grady, Aingeal Rose, 1953-
Love, Miracles & Original Creation: Spiritual Guidance for Understanding Life and Its Purpose
/ Aingeal Rose O'Grady.
Includes bibliographical references (p. 155).

ISBN Paperback: 9781880765791
ISBN eBook: 9781880765784

Cover and Interior Artwork: AHONU.com
Manuscript Editor: AHONU
Manuscript Designer: AHONU.com

First edition published in the USA by Granite Publishing, 2012 as The Nature of Reality
ASIN: B01K3KZSSA under the Wildflower Press imprint.

Address all inquiries to:
Akashic Records Press
an imprint of **Twin Flame Productions LLC**
Via eMail to admin@twinflameproductions.us
Or phone +1-224-588-8026

https://twinflameproduction.us

Warning—Limits of Liability and Disclaimer of Warranty
The author and publisher shall not be liable for your misuse of the material in this book. This book is strictly for informational, educational and entertainment purposes only. The author and/or publisher do not guarantee or warrant that anyone following the techniques, suggestions, tips, ideas, or strategies in this book will become successful at anything. The author and/or publisher shall have neither liability nor responsibility to anyone with respect to any loss or damage howsoever caused, or alleged to be caused, directly or indirectly by the information contained in this book. Always consult a licensed health practitioner for all health issues.